"十四五"职业教育国家规划教材

# 新发展商务英语视听说教程

**特邀主审** 黄大乾
**总 主 编** 何高大

**2**

主 编 周艳芳
副主编 郭晓琳 乐丽萍 刘 敏

北京理工大学出版社
BEIJING INSTITUTE OF TECHNOLOGY PRESS

## 内 容 简 介

《新发展商务英语视听说教程》系列教材是新时代、新文科、新商科背景下，编者深刻把握职业教育面临的新形势、新任务，站位全局，为推动新时代我国职业教育创新发展而精心编写的一部全新理念的职业院校商务英语专业教材。教材编写以商务英语专业学生为教学对象，坚持课程思政、人文性原则、思辨创新性原则和线上线下混合学习原则，融合商务英语素养、语言学习和职业技能，实现知行合一的立体学习目标，旨在提高学生的商务英语能力、职业岗位能力和终身学习能力。

**版权专有　侵权必究**

### 图书在版编目（CIP）数据

新发展商务英语视听说教程 . 2 / 周艳芳主编 . -- 北京：北京理工大学出版社，2021.9（2024.1重印）

ISBN 978-7-5763-0404-6

Ⅰ.①新… Ⅱ.①周… Ⅲ.①商务–英语–听说教学–高等学校–教材 Ⅳ.①F7

中国国家版本馆 CIP 数据核字 (2021) 第 198127 号

---

责任编辑：王晓莉　　文案编辑：王晓莉
责任校对：刘亚男　　责任印制：施胜娟

出版发行 / 北京理工大学出版社有限责任公司
社　　址 / 北京市丰台区四合庄路6号
邮　　编 / 100070
电　　话 / （010）68914026（教材售后服务热线）
　　　　　（010）68944437（课件资源服务热线）
网　　址 / http://www.bitpress.com.cn

版 印 次 / 2024年1月第1版第3次印刷
印　　刷 / 沂南县汶凤印刷有限公司
开　　本 / 889 mm × 1194 mm　1/16
印　　张 / 15
字　　数 / 320千字
定　　价 / 56.80元

图书出现印装质量问题，请拨打售后服务热线，负责调换

# 总　序

"职业教育商务英语专业智慧云版系列教材"是新时代、新文科、新商科背景下，编者们以习近平总书记关于教育的重要论述为行动指南，全面落实《关于深化文化体制改革推动社会主义文化大发展大繁荣若干重大问题的决定》《高等学校课程思政建设指导纲要》《习近平新时代中国特色社会主义思想进课程教材指南》（国教材〔2021〕2号）和中共中央办公厅、国务院办公厅印发《关于推动现代职业教育高质量发展的意见》以及国家教材委员会关于印发《"党的领导"相关内容进大中小学课程教材指南》（国教材〔2021〕5号），学习贯彻党的二十大精神，落实立德树人根本任务，培养德智体美劳全面发展的社会主义建设者和接班人，推动新时代我国商务英语教育创新发展而精心编写的一系列全新理念的职业院校教材。党的十九大的召开，标志着中国社会发展进入新时代。习近平总书记在党的十九大报告中明确提出"完善职业教育和培训体系，坚持产教融合、校企合作"。2021年4月12日全国职业教育大会传达了习近平总书记对职业教育工作作出的重要指示。总书记指示：在全面建设社会主义现代化国家新征程中，职业教育前途广阔、大有可为。要坚持党的领导，坚持正确办学方向，坚持立德树人，优化职业教育类型定位，深化产教融合、校企合作，深入推进育人方式、办学模式、管理体制、保障机制改革，稳步发展职业本科教育，建设一批高水平职业院校和专业，推动职普融通，增强职业教育适应性，加快构建现代职业教育体系，培养更多高素质技术技能人才、能工巧匠、大国工匠。

我国职业技能教育开启了新征程，进入了高质量发展阶段。近年来职业教育接连推出重大政策，职业教育大有可为。2019年，《国家职业教育改革实施方案》首次提出职业教育作为类型教育与普通教育具有同等重要地位；2021年，教育部发布了《本科层次职业教育专业设置管理办法（试行）》（教职成厅〔2021〕1号）；同年，中共中央办公厅、国务院办公厅印发了《关于推动现代职业教育高质量发展的意见》，这表明职业教育发展迎来了春天。新时期职业教育要坚持以习近平新时代中国特色社会主义思想为指导，着眼服务国家现代化建设，推动高质量发展，着力推进改革创新，借鉴先进经验，努力建设高水平、高层次的技术技能人才培养体系。新时期职业教育要瞄准技术变革和产业优化升级的目标，推进产教融合、校企合作，并吸引更多青年接受职业技能教育，促进教育链、人才链与产业链、创新链有效衔接。加强职业学校师资队伍建设，优化办学条件，优化完善教材和教学方式，探索中国特色学徒制，注重学生工匠精神和精益求精习惯的养成，努力培养数以亿计的高素质技术技能人才，为全面建设社会主义现代化国家提供坚实的支撑。

  国际商务最基本的活动是跨国界的经济贸易活动。在信息化3.0时代，深入推进"中国智造"和"中国制造2050"的发展目标，新工艺、新技术、新设备、新材料等将颠覆式地冲击工业、商业、物流、交通、医疗、教育等行业和跨国界的经贸活动，国际贸易结构优化快，知识更新周期缩短，资源配置、服务效率更高。数字商务在国际贸易中的广泛应用，正在掀起国际商务领域里的一场新的变革，商业模式、消费行为的变化导致消费方式变化，疫情催生跨境电商万亿商机。数字商务技术创新，数据资源赋能，新玩家、新玩法、新渠道、新流量、新技术、新市场、新服务等层出不穷。很多的外贸工厂、天猫卖家、Amazon、eBay、全球速卖通、Wish、Shopify和更多传统品牌都改头换面强行进入跨境电商。借助新技术，Amazon上线聊天机器人，推动语音购物。继eBay推出eBay fulfillment 计划之后，其他平台纷纷开通新的物流渠道，如全球速卖通无忧物流、Wish Express、Shopee SLS等。Amazon推出的FBA在提高购物体验、客户忠诚度上成效卓著，之后又迎来了SWA服务，这是跨境电商适应产业互联网时代的又一次商业模式、服务模式的升级，是物流与电商产业高度融合的产物。早期的B2B到B2C将随着产业升级而相映生辉。社交媒体平台TikTok也涉足跨境电商，引领视频直播购物。YouTube Shorts能否使电商规模实现新高，商界也拭目以待。取消各种非关税壁垒，通关和贸易便利化，加快通关和物流配送，提高直邮电商投送时效和客户体验，直邮电商规模也将会创下新高，电商平台涉足物流步伐越来越快，跨境电商结构将得到进一步优化。网经社"电数宝"电商大数据库监测显示，在跨境电商产业链中，主要的进口跨境电商服务平台有天猫国际、京东国际、淘宝全球购、考拉海购、洋码头、苏宁国际、唯品国际、丰趣海淘、蜜芽、宝贝格子、55海淘、别样海外购、亚马逊海外购、五洲会、行云集团、海带网、海拍客、笨土豆等；出口跨境电商有阿里巴巴国际站、亚马逊全球开店、eBay、全球速卖通、Wish、兰亭集势、有棵树、通拓科技、环球资源、敦煌网、大龙网、棒谷、执御、傲基、安克创新、赛维时代等；主要的跨境电商服务商有中国邮政、顺丰速运、京东物流、菜鸟网络、斑马物联网、Paypal、连连支付、一达通、卓志集团等。目前，就市场和资源优势而言，在跨境电商领域，再也没有别的国家比中国具有更大的卖家群体数量和产业规模、更齐全的商业模式和更完备的服务生态，新商科将处在百年未有之大变局。在全球百年未有之大变局下，经济全球化进程遭遇逆流，新冠肺炎疫情已造成全球经济衰退，并将深刻影响经济全球化的发展。我国传统外贸受到了严重冲击，跨境电商却释放出了巨大发展潜力。东盟十国与中国、日本、澳大利亚、新西兰和韩国达成的《区域全面经济伙伴关系协定》（RCEP）于2020年11月正式签署生效，中国与东盟国家进口成本同时下降，这将成为亚洲经济一体化的里程碑，为亚太地区的发展注入了新动力，将构建以国内大循环为主体、国内国际双循环相互促进的新发展格局。职业教育担负着培养数以亿计高素质劳动者的重要任务，让工匠精神真正在职业教育中扎根，为我国由"制造大国"向"智造和智创大国"转型做好人才储备。国际商务格局的巨大变化对职业院校商务英语专业人才培养以及教材建设提出了新的更高要求。应用外语教育必须由重视工具性、技能性、应用性向强化人文性、通识性与创新性、岗位性与职业型、专业与专业集群转型，促进人才的全面发展，对接新型岗位、新型职业和经济社会发展的新需求。

  为了使商务英语教材更好地适应新一轮科技革命和产业变革形势下的国际商务环境，北京理工大学出版社约请我们组织专家和骨干教师编写商务英语专业系列教材。教材编写组进行了前期的调研工作,提炼主题,精心收集相关资料,创新性地推出编写理念新颖、特色鲜明、配套完备的"职业教育商务英语专业智慧云版系列教材"系列丛书,培养适合时代需求的新商科复合型人才。

教材是教师实施课程教学的最基本素材,高质量的教材是教学质量的基本保证。本套教材的编写结合职业教育实际狠抓落实,紧紧围绕党中央,积极响应时代的主题:高举中国特色社会主义伟大旗帜,全面贯彻新时代中国特色社会主义思想,弘扬伟大建党精神,自信自强、守正创新,踔厉奋发、勇毅前行,为全面建设社会主义现代化国家、全面推进中华民族伟大复兴而团结奋斗。深入学习贯彻党的二十大精神,推动党的二十大精神进教材、进课堂、进头脑。本系列教材将思政元素、系统论、金课理念、项目化教材设计三维理论(徐国庆,2020)等运用于教材设计,根据商务英语人才培养方案,吸收行业发展新知识、新技术、新服务,把学习、活动、知识、经验、理论与职业岗位能力、任务整合为项目,凸显"职业维度",体现金课的思政性、高阶性、创新性和挑战度,融合商务英语素养、语言学习和职业技能,实现知行合一的立体学习目标,旨在提高学生中国文化自信、商务英语能力、职业岗位能力和终身的自主学习能力。项目化教材设计三维理论模型如图1所示。

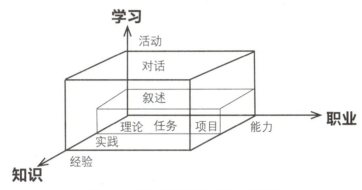

(图1 项目化教材设计三维理论模型)

本系列教材主要遵循以下设计原则:

1. 课程思政、人文性原则。

教材选材得当、主旨性强、体裁多样、题材广泛,符合特定历史时期党和国家的教育方针。本系列教材以专业教学标准和课程内容、任务和成果目标为导向,以立德树人为目标,以商务素养为依托,培养学生的家国情怀,增强学生对祖国的认同感、归属感和自豪感,提升学生思想政治理论素养和文化素养,实现知、情、意、行合一。通过课程思政,了解商务素养与立德树人的内涵,掌握事物发展规律,丰富学识,塑造品格,立志报国,培养学生大担当、大格局、大气魄、大胸襟的人格,使其成为德、智、体、美、劳全面发展的社会主义建设者和接班人。根据每单元的主题,发掘和设计培养学生政治素养、文化素养、商务素养等活动,循序渐进地培养学生的高尚情操、品德和社会责任担当以及厚实的人文基础和商务素养。

2. 能力导向性原则。

本系列教材坚持"以市场为导向、以能力为本位、以就业为根本"的原则,培养学生通晓国际商务知识、跨文化商务交际能力和自主学习能力。"订单式"培养、现代学徒制等已成为职业院校人才培养的创新模式,其核心基于"能力本位",而现代学徒制体现学校、企业"双主体、双导师、双育人"的教学,课程标准与企业的职业岗位标准对接,对接的核心是培养学生的职业能力和岗位技能。本系列教材将基础英语、职业英语、行业英语、产业需要相融合,培养学生未来职业岗位必备的商务英语交际能力和职业能力。本系列教材注重创设商务英语情境，促进语言输入，激发学生已有的文化知识和国际商务知识，引发言说能力和思辨能力，培养岗位实操能力。同时，在实践中，将国家认知、国家认同与国家期待落实到外语教育中，通过外语教育培养符合国家战略需求的人才就是国家立场的体现。引导学生在"学中做、做中学"的过程中，能运用流利的英语讲好中国故事和中国国际商务故事。能力的培养需要知识、实践、应用的衔接，实践高效融合知识传授、能力培养与价值引领，能更好地实现立德树人教学目标。本系列教材还以职业院校的课程衔接为出发点，将教材内容、结构、知识链、产业链有机衔接和贯通，充分体现专业与行业、专业与产业、专业与职业、专业与岗位等不同层次的对接，其核心是提升学生商务英语核心职业能力。学生在语言知识、语言能力、思辨能力提升的过程中，不仅滋养了其高水平的认知需求、增加学业获得感，而且也能满足国家和社会对人才培养的需求，实现教书育人、立德树人的根本目的并彰显了职业外语教育的思政特色。

3. 思辨创新性原则。

批判性思维能力是21世纪劳动者必备能力。本系列教材坚持以学习者为中心，重构课程知识体系、课程能力体系、课程评价体系，强化学生的个性化自主学习能力，培养学生开放、诚信、理性和灵活的品质，学生能辨是非、勤思考、善发现，并愿意运用新观点、新方法去探索更多能解决问题的新途径，尝试更多的新手段，生成更多的新见解。因此，每册书从不同的主题，以问题为切入点，以能力目标为导向，使教学任务具体化、可操作化、目标化和知识结构可视化，培养学生探索、发现、分析、解决问题的能力，激发学生的学习兴趣和创新潜能，让学生主动参与课程学习，掌握"硬技能"，培养计算思维、规则意识、商业实践思想、信息素养、解决复杂问题的综合能力和高级思维能力。为此，教材顺应新时代对商务英语技术技能人才的新要求，精准定位，对接数字经济、科技进步、市场需求，主动适应产业转型升级、新型产业发展和新商科需求，培养学生能用英语讲述中国故事和中国商务故事的同时也能"洋为中用"，运用国际商务知识服务我国的经济社会发展，增强学生建设社会主义现代化强国和实现中华民族伟大复兴中国梦的使命感。

4. 线上线下混合学习原则。

线上线下混合学习是以在线开放课程资源为依托，利用在线教学平台、智慧教学辅助工具，有效地把网络课程教与学（线上）与传统课堂教学（线下）结合起来，进行教与学的活动。线上线下混合学习拓展了教与学的空间，变革了课程和课堂的形态，更有益于个性化学习和多样性教学。本系列教材运用信息化课程、智能化理念和多模态教学设计观，把视频、音频、图片和动画及学习活动整合到线上课程平台，拓展教与学的空间，延伸了主题学习的深度和广度，形成了梯度与挑战度的有机结合，充分体现了线上线下混合学习的优势。

本系列教材特色：

1. 教材以立德树人为根本，坚持"三全育人"，落实立德树人根本任务，积极培育和践行社会主义核心价值观。帮助学生树立正确的世界观、人生观、价值观，培养学生爱国主义情操，提升用英语讲好中国故事、传播好中国声音的能力，坚定文化自信，促进中外文化交流、文明互鉴，为增强中国文化软实力和中华文化世界影响力贡献力量。根据专业人才培养特点、专业能力素质要求结合课程章节内容，梳理思想政治教育元素，提供了课程思政的思路，制定了课程思政的目标：

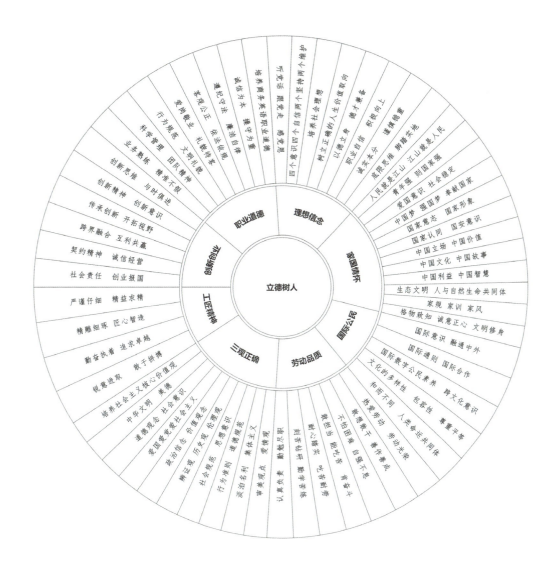

2. 教材以能力本位培养为核心，以"三点一线（切入点、融合点、动情点；思政主线）"为基础，以"具象—循证—释义—融合—评价"的课程思政五步法，以专业知识和技能要点为牵引，基于有效教学证据的循证教学实践，将对学生的价值塑造以专业知识和技能融入由浅入深、循序渐进的知识传授与能力培养之中，激发学生的爱国情、强国志、报国行，起到入耳入脑入心的育人效果，有效解决了课程思政"如何挖掘、如何展现、是否内化"的问题。思政教学目标贯穿于知识、语言、能力、素质以及价值观目标之中。以职业院校学生认知特点为基础，以职场商务英语交际为目标，以商务素养为主线，结合新商科和行业、职业新要求和新特点，精选主题，突出培养学生在未来岗位（群）迫切需要的商务英语能力，注重提升学生商务英语核心职业能力和自主知识构建能力，符合商务英语职业教育的规律和要求。

3. 教材内容设计精细，体现了"起承转合练"的学习特点。每个章节按照教学活动和认知特点，注重选材的时代性、可读性和实用性，内容丰富，形式多样，循序渐进，学练结合。思维导图如画龙点睛，凸显章节学习的核心内容。学习目标（能力、知识、素养、专业能力、方法能力、社会能力），思政目标一表全览，清晰易懂；学评相伴，反思促学；学练活动，生动有趣，旨在学练结合、学以致用。

4. 教材融图片、视频、音频、动画和学习活动为五维一体的课程内容，通过可视、可听、可读、可互动的多模态形式，以经典商务知识和商务活动为依托，通过知识可视化的直观互动性教学，将商务素养融入语言情景学习，实现"学中做、做中学"，提高学生商务知识、语言能力、商务岗位的职业胜任力和创新能力。让学生运用英语完成富有挑战性的真实交际任务，以情景形式展现学习内容，让学生参与和创造情境，在生动的情境中完成商务交际任务，学习语言、训练思维、反思人生观和价值观，实现知识学习、能力提升和立德树人三位一体的教学目标。

5. 教材融合了新知识、新理论、新思维、新技术、新平台、新模式，创新融合课程视听说资源、教学活动资源、主题拓展资源、能力提升资源、智能化竞赛系统和智能化评价系统等资源。这些与学生生活息息相关的多模态资源，不仅能提高学生的学习兴趣，而且可以引发学生情感共鸣，使学生潜移默化地树立正确的意识形态和文化价值观，精神得以涵养，智慧得以启迪，以"润物无声"的方式优化教学过程，提升课程教学质量，实现立德树人目标。这有利于教学模式的变革和创新，有利于有效组织课程教与学、竞赛与评价。教材还配备精心制作的PPT教学课件，教学课件与教材、平台形成一体，相互补充，相得益彰，呈现形式丰富多样，具有可视化、动态化、情景化、智能化和信息化的特点。

本系列教材由我国英语界、商务英语界的知名专家、学者、一线资深教师、行业CEO参与编写和制作。他们中有科研达人和教学改革能手，也有行家高手，能把握当今商务英语发展的脉搏和行业发展的动态。本系列教材包括：

《新发展商务英语视听说教程》（全4册）
《新发展商务英语阅读教程》（全4册）
《新发展商务英语口语教程》（全4册）
《新发展国际商务礼仪英语教程》（全1册）
《新发展商务英语口译教程》（全1册）
《新发展跨境电商英语教程》（全1册）
《新发展商务英语写作教程》（全1册）
《新发展跨文化商务交际英语教程》（全1册）

本系列教材由经验丰富的团队依据先进的职业教学理念编写，具有完整的商务英语职业体系，突出应用性与实践性，关注经济技术发展带来的学习内容与方式的变化，填补了现行新文科、新商科职业院校商务英语专业教材的某些空白。我们深信，本系列教材定能系统丰富学生的商务英语专业知识，全面提升学生商务英语技能、商务素养和创新能力，定能为培养复合型商务英语技术技能型专门人才奠定坚实的基础，定会赢得广大师生的喜爱。

本系列教材能及时出版，我们要特别感谢北京外国语大学博士生导师毛眺源教授、广东白云学院卜玉坤教授、华南农业大学文珊教授、广东理工职业学院彭伟强教授和我们团队的全体编者！同时，我们还要衷心感谢广东省跨境电子商务协会、广州大洋教育科技股份有限公司总裁周春翔先生、广州熙然化妆品有限公司朱昭辉董事长、唯品会（中国）有限公司高级商务经理田静女士，他们为本书的出版给予了极大的帮助和支持！

在编写过程中，我们参考了国内外诸多网站和文献，恕难能一一列举，谨在此深表感谢！由于我们水平有限，如有疏漏或谬误，敬请各位专家、教师不吝赐教，以便我们在再版中改进和完善。

特邀主审　黄大乾　广东白云学院校长、教授、博士

总主编　何高大　教授

# 前 言

英语视听说能力是新时代大学生必备的语言能力。英语视听说课程是大学生的必修课。《新发展商务英语视听说教程 2》（*New Development: Course of Business English—Viewing, Listening and Speaking 2*）是新时代、新文科、新商科背景下，编者深刻把握职业教育面临的新形势、新任务，站位全局，为推动新时代我国职业教育创新发展而精心编写的一部全新理念的职业院校商务英语专业教材。

## 一、编写依据

本教材以习近平总书记关于教育的重要论述为行动指南，全面落实《关于深化文化体制改革推动社会主义文化大发展大繁荣若干重大问题的决定》、《高等学校课程思政建设指导纲要》、《习近平新时代中国特色社会主义思想进课程教材指南》（国教材〔2021〕2号）、中共中央办公厅、国务院办公厅印发《关于推动现代职业教育高质量发展的意见》和国家教材委员会关于印发《"党的领导"相关内容进大中小学课程教材指南》（国教材〔2021〕5号），将系统论、金课理念、项目化设计三维论等运用于教材设计，根据商务英语人才培养方案，吸收行业发展新知识、新技术、新服务，把学习、活动、知识、经验、理论与职业岗位能力、任务整合为项目，凸显"职业维度"，体现金课的高阶性、创新性与挑战度。

本教材以商务英语专业学生为教学对象，坚持课程思政、人文性原则、思辨创新性原则和线上线下混合学习原则，融合商务英语素养、语言学习和职业技能，实现知行合一的立体学习目标；遵循工作过程系统化理念，基于商务领域正常的工作流程开发和设计教材内容，与商务人才的职业能力发展同步，旨在培养学生深刻理解和把握"四个自信""四个意识""两个维护"，提升学生的爱国情怀，提高学生用英语讲好中国故事的能力，提高学生的商务英语语用能力、职业岗位能力和终身学习能力。

## 二、教材特色

本教材通过"视""听""说"三位一体的教学模式，配合背景图片、思维导图和流程图，形成视听说知识可视化和协调互动能力发展的特点，以多模态的形式激发学生的积极性和主动性，提高他们对发生于商务交际场合中的视听材料的理解能力、分析能力、语言表达能力和交际能力，使其具备良好的职业素养和职业道德，能够在具体的工作场合熟练地应用英语聆听他人，表达流畅，问答有礼，并能应对意外情况。依据目前我国职业院校商务英语专业、英语专业学生的实际英语水平、学习要求和现代贸易运营模式变化，本教材着力在教学主题、教学内容、教学方法等方面求新，力图体现以学习者为中心，融"教、学、练、产学研、校企协作、协同育人"为一体的教学理念。本教材在编写理念、内容和任务设计上主要有以下特点：

1. 教材以立德树人为根本，坚持"三全育人"。

落实立德树人根本任务，积极培育和践行社会主义核心价值观，根据专业人才培养特点、专业能力素质要求，梳理思想政治教育元素，提供课程思政的思路。

2. 教材以能力本位培养为核心。

以学生认知特点为基础，以职场商务英语交际为目标，以商务素养为主线，结合新商科、新行业、新职业的要求和特点，精选主题，突出培养学生在未来岗位（群）迫切需要的商务英语能力，注重提升学生商务英语核心职业能力和自主知识构建能力，使其掌握商务英语职业教育的规律。

3. 教材内容设计精细，体现"起承转合练"的循环生态学习特点。

注重时代性、可读性和实用性，内容丰富，形式多样，循环渐进，学练结合。思维导图如画龙点睛，凸显章节学习的核心内容；学习目标（能力、知识、素养、专业能力、方法能力、社会能力）、思政目标一表全览，清晰易懂；学评相伴，反思促学；学练活动，生动有趣，旨在学练结合，学以致用。

4. 教材内容融图片、视频、音频、动画和学习活动为一体。

通过可视、可听、可读、可互动的多模态形式，以经典商务知识和商务活动为依托，通过知识可视化的直观互动性教学，将商务素养融入语言情景学习，实现"学中做、做中学"，提高学生的语言能力、商务岗位的职业胜任力和创新能力。

5. 教材融合新知识、新理论、新思维、新技术、新平台、新模式。

融合课程视听说资源、教学活动资源、主题拓展资源、能力提升资源、智能化竞赛系统和智能化评价系统等资源。配备精心制作的PPT教学课件，教学课件与教材、平台形成一体，具有可视化、动态化、情景化、智能化和信息化课程的特点。

6. 内容安排系统合理、循序渐进。

本套教材共分4册，可以分为初级（Book 1、Book 2）、中级（Book 3）和高级（Book 4），每册供一个学期使用。以培养学生视听说语言基本功为核心，以语言功能、语言情景、职场训练为教学主线系统设计教学内容，内容安排既符合职场新人的成长历程，又符合语言学习的基本规律，结构合理、循序渐进。

### 三、《新发展商务英语视听说教程 2》单元模块设计

本教材分为4大模块，每个模块分为9大工作任务，每个工作任务下又分为4大核心技能，总共144个技能点。每个单元由Overview, Listening Strategies, Lead-in, Business Communication, Project-based Task和Self-assessment Checklist 6个模块组成，每个单元都围绕同一主题展开，与职场情景紧密结合，让学生切身地感受商务英语专业知识技能在职业岗位上的广泛应用和实际效果。

➢ Overview 介绍本单元工作任务所涉及的核心技能点，并配以思维导图，加深学生对本单元核心的了解，把握学习重点，构建学习目标。

➢ Listening Strategies 主要针对性地介绍了听力理解策略和口语策略训练。

➢ Lead-in 包含商务文化背景介绍及热身练习两部分，旨在帮助学生建立背景知识，使其更好地学习本单元内容。

➢ Business Communication 涵盖本单元工作任务所需的4大核心技能点和视听说练习。通过实际的商务情景体现思政特色。

➢ Project-based Task 旨在帮助学生加深对项目、任务过程的理解，通过做中学、学中做的体验模式，强化对本单元技能的掌握。

➢ Self-assessment Checklist 作为形成型评价的核心内容，帮助学生从听力、口语、职业素质3个维度进行反思及评价，全面评价本单元的学习成果，体现了Assessment for Learning的理念，培养学生养成良好的自我反思习惯，找出薄弱环节，及时弥补学习中的不足。这有利于师生及时调整学习策略及教学策略。

### 四、本册各单元素养元素及方法

| 第1单元 | 素养元素 | 素养要点 | 素养方法 | 素养评价 |
| --- | --- | --- | --- | --- |
| 1. Building up strong relationships can help you make a big success in business.<br>2. What will you do after exchanging the contact information with clients?<br>3. Establish contacts.<br>4. Do you mind leaving your business card?<br>5. Introduce business partners.<br>6. I'll send you one of our brochures and then give you a call about prices.<br>7. Keep in touch. | 1. 互利共赢。<br>2. 发展理念。<br>3. 契约精神，诚信共赢。<br>4. 业务熟练。<br>5. 团结协作。<br>6. 精准无误，科学管理。<br>7. 契约精神，诚信共赢。 | 1. 培养学生创新创业精神，发展理念，开拓视野。<br>2. 跨界融合，互利共赢。<br>3. 契约精神，诚信共赢。<br>4. 社会责任。 | 1. 隐性融入法<br>2. 教学设计法<br>3. 行走课堂法<br>4. 启发式教学法<br>5. 探讨式教学法 | 1. 在工作中，学生能掌握商务沟通技巧，与客户顺利沟通交流。<br>2. 在工作中，学生能尊重他人，维护良好的商务关系。<br>3. 在工作中，学生能拥有创新创业精神，诚信共赢，承担社会责任，为合作的顺利开展打下良好的基础。 |

| 第2单元 | 素养元素 | 素养要点 | 素养方法 | 素养评价 |
| --- | --- | --- | --- | --- |
| 1. Introduce business scope.<br>2. We are the market leaders in three countries.<br>3. We have expanded our operations.<br>4. Our company has grown by one-third this year.<br>5. Ask questions about future plan for departments. | 1. 严谨仔细，精益求精。<br>2. 追求卓越、锐意进取、敢于拼搏。<br>3. 创新思维，与时俱进。 | 1. 培养学生工匠精神，严谨仔细，精益求精。<br>2. 精雕细琢，匠心锻造。<br>3. 勤奋执着，追求卓越。<br>4. 锐意进取，敢于拼搏。 | 1. 隐性融入法<br>2. 教学设计法<br>3. 行走课堂法<br>4. 启发式教学法<br>5. 探讨式教学法 | 1. 在工作中，学生拥有严谨仔细，精益求精的精神。<br>2. 在工作中，学生能迎难而上，积极解决问题，追求卓越。<br>3. 在工作中，学生能承担社会责任，锐意进取，敢于拼搏，用发展的眼光看问题。 |
| 第3单元 | 素养元素 | 素养要点 | 素养方法 | 素养评价 |
| 1. I'd like to get all your opinions.<br>2. What can we do to reach this target?<br>3. And we can start thinking about the agenda for the next meeting.<br>4. Now try to disagree with her viewpoints in a confident but polite manner. | 1. 虚心听取。<br>2. 精雕细琢、匠心锻造。<br>3. 谨慎稳重、脚踏实地。<br>4. 包容性，尊重平等，和而不同。 | 1. 培养学生国际公民意识，尊重文化多样性。<br>2. 文化传承、交融与互鉴。<br>3. 包容性，尊重平等。<br>4. 和而不同，美美与共。 | 1. 隐性融入法<br>2. 教学设计法<br>3. 行走课堂法<br>4. 启发式教学法<br>5. 探讨式教学法 | 1. 在工作中，学生能尊重各国文化多样性，包容互鉴。<br>2. 在工作中，学生能注重对本国优秀文化的传承与传播。<br>3. 在工作中，学生能有广阔的胸襟，交融与互鉴，和而不同，美美与共，天下大同。 |
| 第4单元 | 素养元素 | 素养要点 | 素养方法 | 素养评价 |
| 1. I want to meet more challenges in my job.<br>2. like my job very much.<br>3. I follow up customers to make sure they're satisfied with our service.<br>4. After I arrange the trip, I will give you a list to let you know about it.<br>5. Sign a contract. | 1. 锐意进取，敢于拼搏。<br>2. 商务英语职业道德。<br>3. 服务意识。<br>4. 谨慎稳重。<br>5. 契约精神。 | 1. 培养学生优秀的劳动品质，迎难而上，爱岗敬业，关爱客户。<br>2. 礼貌待人，遵守契约。 | 1. 隐性融入法<br>2. 教学设计法<br>3. 行走课堂法<br>4. 启发式教学法<br>5. 探讨式教学法 | 1. 在工作中，学生能具备不畏困难的品质。<br>2. 在工作中，学生能做到爱岗敬业，追求卓越。<br>3. 在工作中，学生能做到全心为客户服务，满足客户需求。<br>4. 待人接物的礼仪，中华民族是礼仪之邦，彬彬有礼是个人名片。 |
| 第5单元 | 素养元素 | 素养要点 | 素养方法 | 素养评价 |
| 1. Asking for check-in information.<br>2. Offering hotel laundry service.<br>3. Pacifying hotel customers. | 1. 文明礼貌，业务熟练，依法依规。<br>2. 职业自信，爱岗敬业，勤勉尽职。<br>3. 尊重平等，克服困难，迎难而上，关爱客户。 | 1. 友善待人，谨慎稳重。<br>2. 关爱客户，遵纪守法。<br>3. 吃苦耐劳，认真负责。<br>4. 服务意识，树立良好的企业形象。 | 1. 隐性融入法<br>2. 教学设计法<br>3. 行走课堂法<br>4. 启发式教学法<br>5. 探讨式教学法 | 1. 在工作中，学生能做到友善待人接物。<br>2. 在工作中，学生能做到爱岗敬业，熟悉工作业务，精益求精，有责任心。<br>3. 在工作中，学生能树立集体主义观点，维护企业形象。 |

| 第6单元 | 素养元素 | 素养要点 | 素养方法 | 素养评价 |
|---|---|---|---|---|
| 1. Business small talk.<br>2. Assigning tasks to subordinates.<br>3. Receive clients at the office. | 1. 积极向上，文化多样性，包容性。<br>2. 尊重平等，严谨仔细，全局意识。<br>3. 业务熟练，关爱客户，诚信共赢，锐意进取，敢于拼搏。 | 1. 人际交往，善于沟通。<br>2. 正确的三观。<br>3. 认真负责，及时反馈。<br>4. 大局意识，国际合作，职业精神，发展理念。 | 1. 隐性融入法<br>2. 教学设计法<br>3. 行走课堂法<br>4. 启发式教学法<br>5. 探讨式教学法 | 1. 在工作中，学生能掌握商务沟通技巧，与客户顺利沟通交流。<br>2. 在工作中，学生能正确处理上下级关系，尊重平等，维护良好的同事关系。<br>3. 在工作中，学生能关爱客户，了解客户喜好，为合作的顺利开展打下良好的基础。 |
| 第7单元 | 素养元素 | 素养要点 | 素养方法 | 素养评价 |
| 1. Show clients around the company.<br>2. Welcome visitors, accompany visitors while expecting.<br>3. Pay attention to visitors' interests and answer their questions. | 1. 求真精神，劳动精神，职业道德。<br>2. 职业素养，人文关怀，服务意识。<br>3. 职业精神，契约精神。 | 1. 实事求是，认真负责，诚信经营。<br>2. 树立企业品牌形象，展现企业文化和精神风貌。<br>3. 主动了解客户需求，促进深度合作。 | 1. 隐性融入法<br>2. 教学设计法<br>3. 行走课堂法<br>4. 启发式教学法<br>5. 探讨式教学法 | 1. 在工作中，学生能形成实事求是、诚信经营的品格。<br>2. 学生能学会礼貌待人，给客户留下良好印象，展现专业的企业形象。<br>3. 学生能学会观察客户需求，提供专业解答，促进商业合作的成功达成。 |
| 第8单元 | 素养元素 | 素养要点 | 素养方法 | 素养评价 |
| 1. Motivate clients before signing the contract.<br>2. Plan a special and customized entertaining activity for your clients.<br>3. Bond with clients through exchanging personal information. | 1. 职业精神，合作精神，创新创业。<br>2. 职业道德，劳动品质。<br>3. 社会主义核心价值观，以人为本，合作精神。 | 1. 进取精神，推动合作共赢。<br>2. 爱岗敬业，关爱客户，认真负责。<br>3. 人际交往，消除隔阂，促进互利共赢。 | 1. 隐性融入法<br>2. 教学设计法<br>3. 行走课堂法<br>4. 启发式教学法<br>5. 探讨式教学法 | 1. 学生能认识到招待客户对商业合作达成的重要性。<br>2. 学生能学会了解客户个人偏好，制定个性化服务。<br>3. 学生能掌握商务沟通技巧，拉进与客户之间的距离，向商务伙伴展现积极良好的合作态度。 |
| 第9单元 | 素养元素 | 素养要点 | 素养方法 | 素养评价 |
| 1. People are suffering from loads of stress from their jobs.<br>2. How can we deal with work stress in a healthy way?<br>3. One of the best ways to deal with workplace stress is to find someone to talk about the problems. | 1. 社会主义核心价值观，社会责任，中华美德。<br>2. 时代精神，生命教育，心理健康教育；人与自然生命共同体教育。<br>3. 价值观念，理想信念，创新创业。 | 1. 民主、文明、和谐、友善，关爱自我，关爱他人。<br>2. 坚韧不拔，自强不息，危机应对意识和方法。<br>3. 敢担当、能吃苦、肯奋斗；正确人生价值取向，职业观。 | 1. 隐性融入法<br>2. 教学设计法<br>3. 行走课堂法<br>4. 启发式教学法<br>5. 探讨式教学法 | 1. 学生能认识到工作压力的危害和心理健康的重要性。<br>2. 学生能掌握正确处理工作压力的方法和手段。<br>3. 学生能树立健康向上、积极乐观的职业观和生活态度，正确把握工作与生活的平衡。<br>4. 尊重自然、顺应自然，构建人与自然生命共同体。 |

建议以"三点一线（切入点、融合点、动情点；思政主线）"为基础，以"具象—循证—释义—融合—评价"的课程思政五步法，以专业知识和技能要点为牵引，基于有效教学证据的循证教学实践，将对学生的价值塑造以专业知识和技能融入由浅入深、循序渐进的知识传授与能力培养之中，激发学生的爱国情、强国志、报国行，起到入耳入脑入心的育人效果，有效解决课程思政"如何挖掘、如何展现、是否内化"的问题。思政教学目标贯穿于知识、语言、能力、素质以及价值观目标之中。

本书由何高大教授担任总主编，负责教程的总体策划、体例设计、主题确定、部分内容编写、统稿、审校、智慧云、APP设计等组织管理和编写工作，周艳芳副教授担任主编，郭晓琳、乐丽萍、刘敏老师担任副主编。广州熙然化妆品有限公司朱昭辉董事长、广州大洋教育信息技术有限公司总裁周春翔先生、广东头狼教育科技有限公司朱加宝董事长等对本书的编写提供了许多来自岗位一线的案例和语料，并提供了诸多建设性建议，在此表示对他们真诚的感谢！

在编写过程中陈玉嫣、赵清宁老师帮助提供了素材，在此我们表示最诚挚的感谢！同时我们还参考了诸多文献和网站，限于篇幅，恕未能一一列出，在此表示真诚的谢意！

由于我们才疏识浅，难免存在纰漏，敬请读者和相关院校在使用过程中给予关注和批评指正，以便及时修订和加以完善。在此表示真诚的感谢！

编　者

2021 年 8 月

# 目 录

### Unit 1 Building up Business Relationships

| | |
|---|---|
| Overview | 2 |
| Listening Strategies | 4 |
| Lead-in | 6 |
| Business Communication | 8 |
| Project-based Task | 20 |
| Self-assessment Checklist | 23 |

### Unit 2 Introducing Companies

| | |
|---|---|
| Overview | 26 |
| Listening Strategies | 28 |
| Lead-in | 31 |
| Business Communication | 33 |
| Project-based Task | 44 |
| Self-assessment Checklist | 47 |

### Unit 3 Attending Meetings

| | |
|---|---|
| Overview | 50 |
| Listening Strategies | 52 |
| Lead-in | 55 |
| Business Communication | 57 |
| Project-based Task | 69 |
| Self-assessment Checklist | 72 |

## Unit 4
### Traveling on Business

| | |
|---|---|
| Overview | 74 |
| Listening Strategies | 76 |
| Lead-in | 78 |
| Business Communication | 80 |
| Project-based Task | 94 |
| Self-assessment Checklist | 96 |

## Unit 5
### Staying at a Hotel

| | |
|---|---|
| Overview | 98 |
| Listening Strategies | 100 |
| Lead-in | 102 |
| Business Communication | 105 |
| Project-based Task | 119 |
| Self-assessment Checklist | 122 |

## Unit 6
### Receiving Clients

| | |
|---|---|
| Overview | 124 |
| Listening Strategies | 126 |
| Lead-in | 128 |
| Business Communication | 130 |
| Project-based Task | 144 |
| Self-assessment Checklist | 146 |

## Unit 7 Showing Clients Around the Company

- Overview ········· 148
- Listening Strategies ········· 150
- Lead-in ········· 153
- Business Communication ········· 155
- Project-based Task ········· 169
- Self-assessment Checklist ········· 172

## Unit 8 Entertaining Clients

- Overview ········· 174
- Listening Strategies ········· 176
- Lead-in ········· 178
- Business Communication ········· 180
- Project-based Task ········· 193
- Self-assessment Checklist ········· 195

## Unit 9 Dealing with Stress

- Overview ········· 198
- Listening Strategies ········· 200
- Lead-in ········· 202
- Business Communication ········· 204
- Project-based Task ········· 217
- Self-assessment Checklist ········· 219

## Overview

Building up strong relationships can help you make a big success in business. It could happen when we meet our clients in the offices, business parties, important meetings or some casual meetings. Sometimes we've got important business to take care of, but sometimes all we need to do is to say hello, introduce ourselves and exchange business cards. With an appropriate introduction, a positive attitude and great confidence, you can find yourself creating a favorable impression and establishing friendly relationships. Therefore, in this unit, we will learn **how to establish contacts with new clients, introduce business partners, talk about business/products, and keep in touch.** Now let us start our business journey!

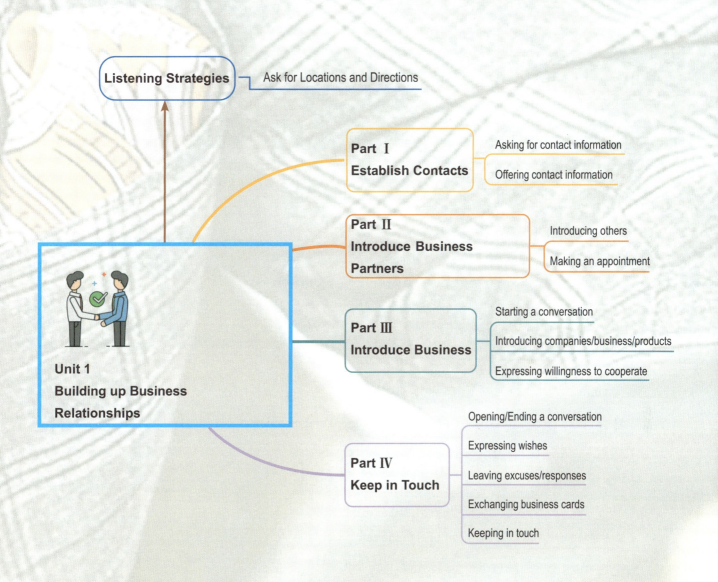

# Listening Strategies

## Understanding Locations and Directions (1)

It is necessary for us to listen for the information about locations and directions, especially when we are on a business trip. In this part, we will learn how to ask for locations and directions in English. Here are three steps.

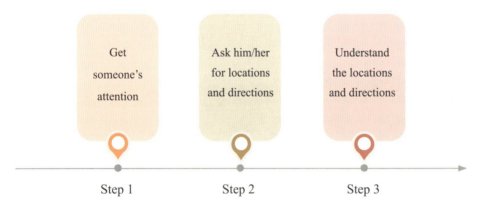

Here are some typical expressions to ask for locations and directions.

### Ask for Locations and Directions

1. Excuse me! Could you tell me the way to the museum?
2. Pardon me! I'm lost. How can I get to the café?
3. Please tell me how I could get to your apartment.
4. Excuse me! Is there a park nearby?
5. What's the best way to the supermarket?
6. Excuse me! Do you know where the library is?
7. Could you help me, please? I'm looking for the bank.
8. Can you show me Guangzhou on the map?
9. How far is it to the airport?
10. Is it far (from here)/a long way?

Unit 1 | Building up Business Relationships

## Task

Listen to the conversation and fill in the blanks. You can try to draw a map to help you get the locations and directions.

### Conversation 1

Jane: Excuse me! _____ do I get to the _____?

Mary: Sorry, I'm not from around here.

Jane: _____ where the closest bus station is?

Mary: If you _____ the street, you'll _____ a bus station there!

Jane: Thank you.

Mary: Don't mention it.

### Conversation 2

Tom: Excuse me! _____ the exhibition?

Lin: This way. Go straight ahead. Turn right at the traffic lights. _____ the street. Walk past the park, and keep going straight _____ you see the sign for the exhibition.

Tom: Great! Thanks for your help.

Lin: You're welcome.

### Conversation 3

Tourist: Sorry to trouble you, but _____ locate this _____ written in the book *60 Beijing Road*.

Stranger: Zoo? Oh. You've come to the right person! I know it exactly.

Tourist: Great! Can you please tell me _____ there?

Stranger: OK. Look, _____ down this street directly for 2 blocks. Then turn _____ at Shanghai Avenue. Go straight on until you find the zoo. It's on the right side of the Avenue. You won't miss it.

Tourist: Is there any landmark (地标) by the zoo?

Stranger: It's near the Kung Fu Restaurant.

Tourist: _____ does it _____ to go to the zoo from here on foot?

Stranger: It's not far. It is about _____.

Tourist: Thank you very much. You are so kind.

Stranger: It's my pleasure.

# Lead-in

## Cultural Background

"Results depend on relationships." Don Petersen said. He is the ex-CEO of America's Ford Motor Company (福特汽车公司). Business is all about relationships. Good business relationships will help you get the results you want. The stronger relationships you have, especially with customers or clients, the more successful you'll be. So, you will find that being able to make small talk (闲聊；聊天)—especially before a business meeting—is helpful for you to build good relationships.

Building up business relationships includes meeting people and talking to them, sharing contact information, helping each other and ultimately (最终) getting new business. You can introduce yourself and talk about your company. Ask them about their business and what they do. Then explain a bit about what you do and who uses your products. If it's appropriate, tell them you may be able to meet their needs. Then see if they would consider purchasing the products from you. Just be sincere and friendly.

Unit 1 | Building up Business Relationships

### Task 1 ▶

Read the above passage and answer the following questions.

1. If you are not good at building up business relationships, what can you do?
2. How can good business relationships help us?

### Task 2 ▶

Think about the following questions and discuss in small groups.

1. What do you need to do when meeting new clients?
2. What will you do after exchanging the contact information with clients?

# Warm-up

### Task ▶

When you saw the phrase "business relationships", what's the first word that occurs to you? Maybe "conversation" or "trust", etc. Let's have a brainstorm and draw a mind map together. List anything that you think is related to the key word "business relationships", and put them in the circles. Feel free to use some colorful mark pens to help your mind map look better. After drawing, please share your mind map with your classmates.

# Business Communication

## Part Ⅰ Establish Contacts

    In this part, you will hear a business conversation between two native speakers. They introduce themselves and exchange basic information in the conversation. This part consists of 3 activities. After each listening task, some useful language points will be discussed and you might use them in the following speaking task.

### Words and Expressions

| | | | |
|---|---|---|---|
| industries | /ˈɪndəstriz/ | n. | the people or companies engaged in a particular kind of commercial enterprise 行业，工业；实务公司（industry的复数） |
| establish | /ɪˈstæblɪʃ/ | v. | to set up or lay the groundwork for 建立，确立；创立 |
| exhibition | /ˌeksɪˈbɪʃn/ | n. | the act of exhibiting; a collection of things (goods or works of art etc.) for public display 展览，显示；展览会 |
| sales department | | | the division of a business that is responsible for selling products or services 业务部，（贸易）营业部；销售部 |

### Activity 1　Extensive Listening

Listen to the conversation and decide whether the following statements are true (T) or false (F).

1. Mr. Brown is the import manager of Atlantic Industries Ltd. （　　）
2. Mr. Brown has found something interesting. （　　）
3. Mr. Brown and Ms. Anderson exchanged their business cards. （　　）

## Activity 2 | Intensive Listening

### Task 1

Listen to the conversation again and answer the following questions.

1. What company does Mr. Brown work for?
2. What's the first name of the female speaker?
3. Do they meet for the first time?

### Task 2

Listen to the conversation again and fill in the blanks with no more than three words.

A: Good afternoon, sir. May I know what _____ you are from?

B: I'm Matt Brown, the import manager of Atlantic Industries Ltd., Sydney, Australia.

A: Good afternoon, Mr. Brown. My name is Juliet Anderson, the manager of the _____.

B: _____ to see you, Ms. Anderson.

A: Did you find anything _____?

B: I'm just _____ here. I haven't seen as much as I could.

A: Would you mind leaving your _____ here?

B: No. I'd be glad to. Here is my card.

A: Thank you. And here's _____. Please call me anytime if there's anything I can do for you.

## Activity 3 | Speaking

### Language Bank

When meeting a client for the first time, you might need to establish contacts with him/her for future cooperation (合作). Here are some common expressions you might use.

**Asking for contact information:**

May I know/Can I ask what company you are from?

Do you mind leaving your business card?

May/Can I have your business card?

Here's my card. Do you have a business card?

**Offering contact information:**

I'm ×××, from the… (company's name), … (city, country).

My name is ×××, … (job title) of the… (company's name).

Use the expressions above. Create your own business conversation and practice it with your partner.

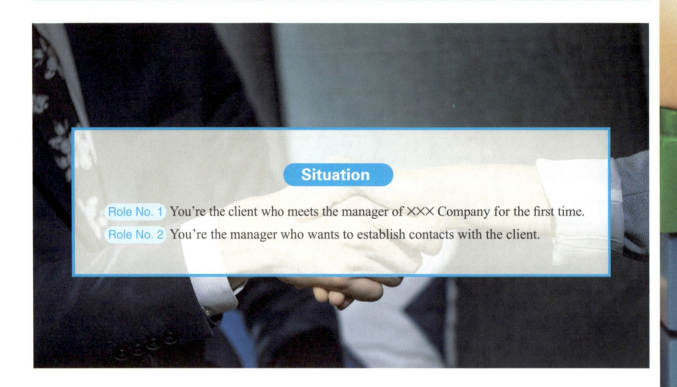

**Situation**

Role No. 1 You're the client who meets the manager of ××× Company for the first time.

Role No. 2 You're the manager who wants to establish contacts with the client.

# Part II  Introduce Business Partners

In this part, you will hear a business conversation among several businessmen. They introduce business partners. This part consists of 3 activities. After each listening task, some useful language points will be discussed and you might use them in the following speaking task.

| | | | Words and Expressions |
|---|---|---|---|
| buddy | /ˈbʌdɪ/ | n. | a close friend who accompanies his buddies in their activities 伙伴, 好朋友; 密友 |
| import | /ˈimpɔːt/ | n. | commodities (goods or services) bought from a foreign country 进口; 进口货; 输入 |
| seize | /siːz/ | v. | to take hold of; to grab; to take or capture by force 抓住; 夺取; 理解; 逮捕 |

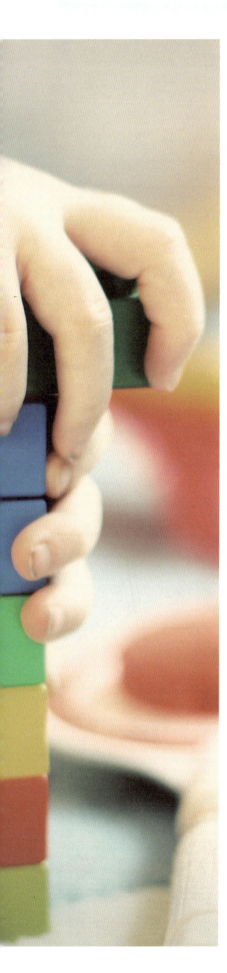

Unit 1 | Building up Business Relationships

## Activity 1   Extensive Listening

Listen to the conversation and decide whether the following statements are true (T) or false (F).

1. Wang Ming and John are friends.   (   )
2. Wang Ming and Tim Alexander met for the first time.   (   )
3. John's company is doing business with importing toys.   (   )

## Activity 2   Intensive Listening

### Task 1

Listen to the conversation again and answer the following questions.

1. Did Tim Alexander and Wang Ming close the deal this time?
2. What did Tim Alexander say about meeting at ten tomorrow morning?
3. What does Tim Alexander's company do?

### Task 2

Listen to the conversation again and fill in the blanks with no more than three words.

John: Oh, by the way, I would like you to _____ my friend, Ming. Ming, this is my buddy, Tim.

Wang Ming: Nice to meet you. I'm Wang Ming.

Tim Alexander: Me, too. I'm Tim Alexander. Just _____ me Tim.

John: Well, Tim's company is _____ with importing toys. Maybe you can seize the opening.

Wang Ming: Of course, thank you so much, John. And I think we should have a _____ sometime later. Do you think so, Tim?

Tim Alexander: Good idea. It _____ me.

Wang Ming: Then let's make it tomorrow morning. Say ten?

Tim Alexander: OK, I will come to the booth to meet you.

## Activity 3　Speaking

### Language Bank

In the process of seeking new business partners and building up business relationships, your clients could come from others' introduction. Here are some common expressions that might help you.

**Introducing others:**

I would like you to know my buddy/friend…, ×××.

×××, this is my buddy/friend…, ×××.

×××'s company is doing business with…

**Making an appointment:**

I think we should have a further talk sometime later. Do you think so?

Let's make it…/Say…?

I will come to the… to meet you.

Use the expressions above. Create your own business conversation and practice it with your partner.

### Situation

Role No. 1　You want to introduce a new client to your business partner, ×××.

Role No. 2　You're meeting with your business partner in a coffee shop, and he/she is going to introduce a new client.

# Part III  Introduce Business

It's a big day of the International Plastics Conference. Anna and the rest of the Tip Top Trading team are at the International Plastics Conference and looking to promote their business. Will Anna be able to network (建立关系) and make some useful contacts at the conference?

| Words and Expressions | | | |
|---|---|---|---|
| executive | /ɪgˈzekjʊtɪv/ | n. | someone who is employed by a business at a senior level, decide what the business should do, and ensure that it is done 执行总监 |
| chatty | /ˈtʃætɪ/ | a. | someone who is chatty talks a lot in a friendly, informal way 爱闲聊的 |
| wedge | /wedʒ/ | n. | A wedge of something such as fruit or cheese is a piece of it that has a thick triangular shape. 楔形物 |
| plastic | /ˈplæstɪk/ | n. | Plastic is a material that is produced from oil by a chemical process and that is used to make many objects. It is light in weight and does not break easily. 塑料 |
| mouldy | /ˈməʊldɪ/ | a. | Something that is mouldy is covered with mould. 发霉的 |
| brochure | /ˈbrəʊʃə(r)/ | n. | a thin magazine with pictures that gives you information about a product or service 小册子 |

## Activity 1  Extensive Watching

Watch a short video and answer the following questions.

1. What are they mainly talking about in this conversation?
2. Do they sell the same products?
3. Have they exchanged their contact details?

## Activity 2  Intensive Watching

### Task 1

Watch the video again and choose the correct answers.

1. What does Anna do at Tip Top Trading?

   A. CEO.　　　　　　　　　　　　B. Sales Executive.

   C. Manager.　　　　　　　　　　D. Advertising (广告) Executive.

2. What is the product of Tip Top Trading?

   A. Plastic fruit.　　B. Cheese.　　C. Fresh grapes.　　D. Cake.

### Task 2

Watch the video again and fill in the blanks.

Anna: Oh yes, of course. So can you tell me about your _____, Nice' n' Cheesy?

Jane: Well, we _____ cheese to London's top cheese shops—we like to say we're a wedge above the rest—a wedge of cheese, get it?!

Anna: Err, right. Well, can I _____ tell you about what our company does? Our company—Tip Top Trading—makes plastic fruit mainly for the catering and food _____. We're up for an award today for one of our _____.

Jane: Smashing (了不起的，极好的). That's quite interesting actually. We have an issue with the fresh grapes we provide with our cheeses—they keep going mouldy.

Anna: Oh dear.

Jane: Yes—sour grapes you could say! A good _____ plastic grape would be useful to _____ our cheese displays.

Anna: Well, I think we might be able to _____ you.

## Activity 3　Speaking

## Language Bank

If you want to make some useful contacts at the conference and promote your business, you can use some common expressions as follows.

**Starting a conversation:**

Excuse me, hello, I'm ×××. I work as a… (job title) at… (company's name), and you are…?
It's very busy here today, isn't it?

**Introducing companies/business/products:**

Can you tell me about your company… (company's name)?

Unit 1 | Building up Business Relationships 15

Can I briefly tell you about what our company does?

We sell/focus on/make… (product) mainly for… industry.

Our company specializes in/focuses on… (product).

**Expressing willingness to cooperate:**

I think we might be able to help you.

I'll send you one of our brochures and then give you a call about prices.

## Task 1 ▶

Use the expressions you've just learned as prompts and watch the video again. Then practice the conversation with your partner.

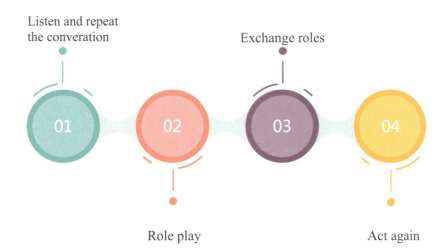

01 Listen and repeat the conversation

02 Role play

03 Exchange roles

04 Act again

## Task 2 ▶

Use the expressions above. Create your own business conversation and practice it with your group members.

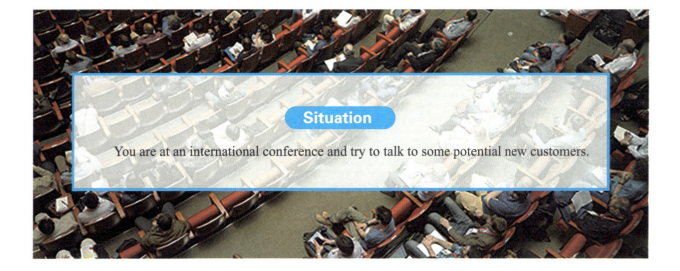

**Situation**

You are at an international conference and try to talk to some potential new customers.

# Part IV  Keep in Touch

In this part, you will watch a short video about conversations among some native speakers. In the video, they all dress formally and seem to have a great time. This part consists of 3 tasks. After each watching and listening task, some useful language points will be discussed and you might use them in the following speaking task.

## Words and Expressions

| | | | |
|---|---|---|---|
| pleasure | /ˈpleʒə(r)/ | n. | something or someone that provides pleasure; a source of happiness 快乐；希望；娱乐 |
| conference | /ˈkɒnfərəns/ | n. | a prearranged meeting for consultation or exchange of information or discussion (especially one with a formal agenda) 会议；讨论；协商 |
| toast | /təʊst/ | n. | a drink in honor of or to the health of a person or event 干杯；接受敬酒的人 |
| keep in touch | | | to maintain contact with another person 保持联络 |
| look…up | | | to contact someone, typically when you are in the area where they live 联系；拜访 |
| Bon voyage | | | You say "bon voyage" to someone who is going on a journey, as a way of saying goodbye and wishing them a good trip. 一路平安 |

## Activity 1  Extensive Watching

Watch a short video and answer the following questions.

1. Where did this conversation take place?
2. How many people are there in this conversation?
3. Do these speakers work in the same company? How do you know?

Unit 1 | Building up Business Relationships    17

## Activity 2   Intensive Watching

### Task 1

Watch the video again and choose the correct answers.

1. How did Victor go home?
   A. By bus.    B. By plane.    C. By boat.    D. By bike.
2. Who proposed a toast at the party?
   A. Sam.    B. Lin.    C. Victor.    D. The waiter.

### Task 2

Watch the video again and fill in the blanks.

(V=Victor, S=Sam, L=Lin, W=Waiter)

V: Well, it has been a great _____ to meet you, Sam and Lin.

S: Yes. We've _____ meeting you too, Victor.

L: Yes, it's been great. What a _____ you have to go home!

V: Well, all good things must come to an _____, but I'm sure we'll meet again.

S: Yes, I hope so.

L: And good luck with your business. I'm sure it will go well.

V: And I wish you every _____, too.

S: Well, I think we should drink a toast to the end of the conference and to ourselves. Here's to us.

L: Cheers.

    …

S: We should keep in _____.

V: Yes. Have I given you my card?

S: No. Thanks very much. Here's mine.

V: Do you have a card, Lin?

L: Yes.

V: Thank you. I'll send you an _____. And if you're ever in Singapore, you must _____.

S: We certainly will. And you have my number. When you're next in Sydney, give me a call. We'll have a drink.

W: May I take this?

V: Well, I'd better get going or I'll miss my _____.

S: Have a good flight home. Bon voyage.

L: Good bye. Until next time.

V: Good bye.

## Activity 3  Speaking

## Language Bank

When socializing at a business party with someone, you can use some common expressions as follows.

**Opening/Ending a conversation:**

It has been a great pleasure to meet you.
I've enjoyed meeting you, too.
I'm pleased to meet you.
Pleasure is mine.

**Expressing wishes:**

Good luck with your business.
Wish you every success.
Wish you all the best.

**Leaving excuses:**

All (good) things must come to an end.
I'd better go, or I'll…

**Leaving responses:**

What a pity you have to go (home)!
I'm sure we'll meet again.

**Exchanging business cards:**

Do you have a card?
Have I given you my card?
Here's my card.

**Keeping in touch:**

If you're ever in…, you must look me up.
When you're next in…, give me a call. We'll have a drink/meetup.
You have my number.
We'll keep in touch.

Unit 1 | Building up Business Relationships

## Task 1 ▶

Use the expressions you've just learned to complete the following conversation. Then practice it with your partner.

A: Nice evening. And I'm very _____ to _____ you again, Mr. Smith. Cheers to the event and ourselves.

B: Pleasure is all mine, Mr. Wang. Cheers.

B: I'm really _____ meeting you tonight. Unfortunately, I must _____ or I will _____ my flight.

A: Well, if you're ever in Beijing, remember to give me _____. You have my _____.

B: I certainly will. And I _____ you every success.

A: You too. Have a _____ flight.

B: Thanks. See you next time.

## Task 2 ▶

Use the expressions above. Create your own business conversation and practice it with your group members.

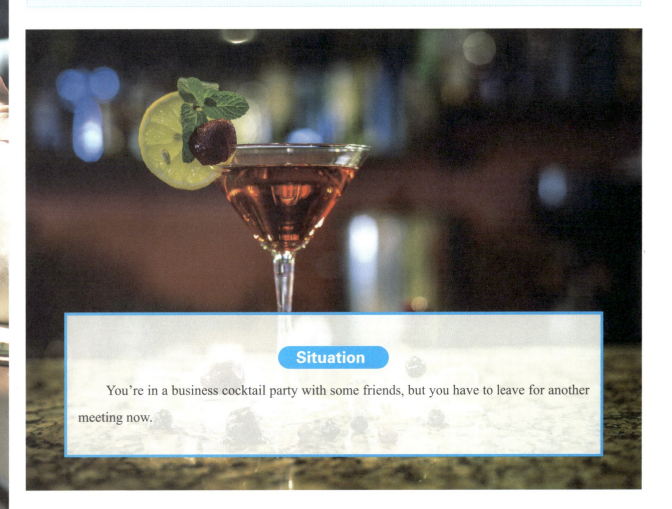

**Situation**

You're in a business cocktail party with some friends, but you have to leave for another meeting now.

# Project-based Task

## Objectives

1. Exchange contact information and establish contacts with new clients
2. Introduce business partners and make an appointment
3. Introduce business or products, and express willingness to cooperate
4. Express wishes, exchange business cards and keep in touch

## Task Background

It's a big day of the International ABC Conference and a good opportunity for businessmen in the toy industry to promote their business. Mary and her team are at the conference and they want to find some potential clients.

## Procedures

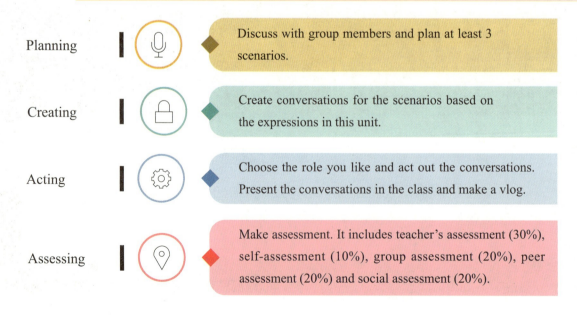

Planning — Discuss with group members and plan at least 3 scenarios.

Creating — Create conversations for the scenarios based on the expressions in this unit.

Acting — Choose the role you like and act out the conversations. Present the conversations in the class and make a vlog.

Assessing — Make assessment. It includes teacher's assessment (30%), self-assessment (10%), group assessment (20%), peer assessment (20%) and social assessment (20%).

## Possible Scenarios

### Scenario 1

Mary and her team have arrived early at the International ABC Conference, looking for some potential clients. They heard that the CEO of ××× Company is also at the conference and they didn't want to miss the opportunity. So, firstly, they go there and establish contacts.

Role No. 1  Mary: Introduce herself and exchange business card...

Role No. 2  Mary's teammate A

Role No. 3  Mary's teammate B

Role No. 4  CEO of ××× Company: Introduce himself and exchange business cards...

...

( Role No. 5  the assistant of the CEO )

*Body gestures like handshake and items like business cards must be included.

### Scenario 2

After establishing contacts, Mary would also like to introduce her teammates who are so intelligent and helpful. And they also need to introduce their business.

Role No. 1  Mary: Introduce the teammates one by one, including job titles and duties; introduce the business...

Role No. 2  Mary's teammate A: Introduce himself...

Role No. 3  Mary's teammate B: Introduce herself...

Role No. 4  CEO of ××× Company: Ask questions about Mary's business...

...

( Role No. 5  the assistant of the CEO )

## Scenario 3

Mary and the CEO of ×××Company are having a good time. They want to have a further talk but the CEO of ×××Company is going to give a speech at the conference. So, they arrange the next meeting and promise to keep in touch.

Role No. 1 Mary: Ask about the next meeting; keep in touch…

Role No. 2 Mary's teammate A: Keep in touch/say goodbye…

Role No. 3 Mary's teammate B: Keep in touch/say goodbye…

Role No. 4 CEO of ×××Company: Give a leaving excuse; arrange next meeting; keep in touch…

…

( Role No. 5 the assistant of the CEO )

Requirements:

- All group members are required to take part in the project.
- Use the expressions you have learned in this unit as many as possible.

# Self-assessment Checklist

Now, it's time for you to review your performance after learning this unit. Carry out a self-assessment by checking the following table.

| Items | | Ratings | | | |
|---|---|---|---|---|---|
| | | A | B | C | D |
| Listening Skills | I can recognize the expressions about locations and directions. | | | | |
| | I can get contact information. | | | | |
| | I can understand greetings and introductions at the business party. | | | | |
| | I can catch the information about a business appointment. | | | | |
| | I can understand business and products. | | | | |
| | I can understand reasons for leaving. | | | | |
| | I can understand willingness to cooperate. | | | | |
| | I can understand good wishes. | | | | |
| Speaking Skills | I can ask for the information about locations and directions. | | | | |
| | I can greet someone and introduce myself. | | | | |
| | I can ask for and offer contact information. | | | | |
| | I can introduce other people at the business party. | | | | |
| | I can make a business appointment. | | | | |
| | I can talk about business and products. | | | | |
| | I can express my willingness to cooperate. | | | | |
| | I can express good wishes. | | | | |
| Professional Skills | I can establish good business relationships with new clients. | | | | |
| | I can introduce business partners to other people to expand business relationships. | | | | |
| | I can talk about business products or service to maintain relationships. | | | | |
| | I can keep further business relationships with clients after we separate with each other. | | | | |

A: Basically agree

B: Agree

C: Strongly agree

D: Disagree

# Unit 2

# Introducing Companies

# Overview

The image of your company plays an essential role in attracting your potential business partners for further cooperation. You may need to present your company to visitors, investors, partners, new suppliers or clients. What can you talk about your company? How would you describe it? There are a number of things to consider. For instance, the company history, its employees, and its branches. And there are also company departments, culture, reputation, and future plans. In this unit, we will focus on **how to introduce business scope, employees, company history and departments.** Now let us start our business journey!

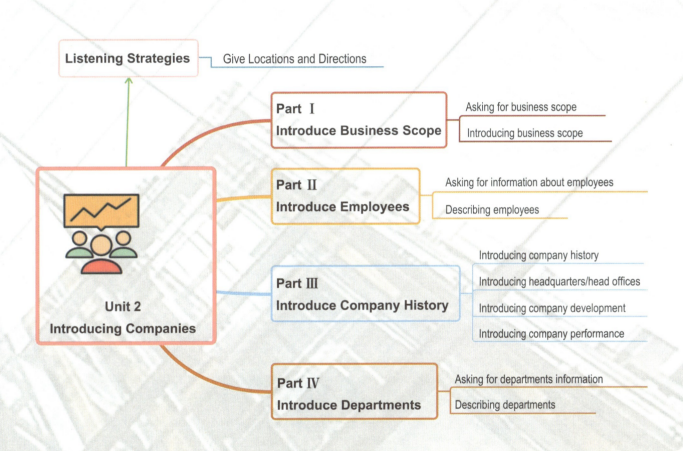

# Listening Strategies

## Understanding Locations and Directions (2)

In Unit 1, we have learned how to ask for locations and directions in English when we want to know where a place or building is. Now think about how to give locations and directions to other people who ask you for help. Here are three tips.

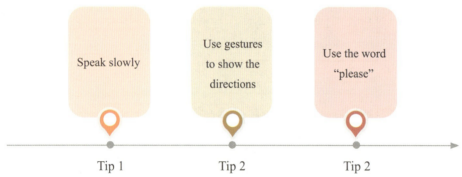

Tip 1 — Speak slowly
Tip 2 — Use gestures to show the directions
Tip 2 — Use the word "please"

We often use some verbs and prepositions to describe locations and directions. Look at the following pictures.

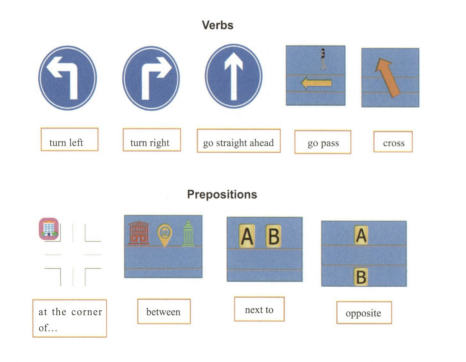

**Verbs**: turn left, turn right, go straight ahead, go pass, cross

**Prepositions**: at the corner of..., between, next to, opposite

Here are some typical expressions to give locations and directions.

## Give Locations and Directions

1. Take the first/second left/right.
2. Turn right at the crossroads.
3. Keep going straight ahead and you will see it on the right.
4. Continue straight ahead for about a mile.
5. Take a left at the junction.
6. Take the first right when you enter Steven Street.
7. Take the second exit at the T-junction and then turn right at the traffic lights.
8. This straight road will lead you to the library.
9. The shop is between the supermarket and KFC.
10. Drive to Xueyuan Street and turn left.

## Task

Listen to the conversation and fill in the blanks. You can try to draw a map to help you get the locations and directions.

### Conversation 1

Rose: Excuse me! Is there a _____ near here?

Mike: Yes, there's one near here.

Rose: _____ is it to the library?

Mike: It's not far, maybe about _____.

Rose: Could you please _____ me?

Mike: It's that way. Go straight ahead. _____ at the junction. This straight road will _____ you _____ the library.

### Conversation 2

Amy: Can you give me _____ to the Beijing Restaurant?

Tom: Yes, sure. Do you know the _____?

Amy: Yes.

Tom: When you get to the supermarket, take the _____. You'll pass a museum. The Beijing Restaurant is _____ the museum.

Amy: Thank you very much.

Tom: Be careful. There are many schools _____.

Amy: I really want to thank you for your help.

Tom: Not at all.

### Conversation 3

Jack: Do you know how to _____ the gallery? I've never been there before.

Michael: Certainly. However, there might still be road repairs (修路). You should be careful.

Jack: Thanks for your _____.

Michael: _____ this street for two blocks and turn left. _____ ahead and you will see a park. _____ when you see the park. Go down there. The gallery is between a bookstore and a garden.

Jack: Thank you again. Have a nice day.

## Cultural Background

Since the earliest days, humans have been cooperating and trading to create wealth and gain access to (获得使用……的机会) goods and services in various ways. People exchanged their things to meet their needs. For example, a hunter traded meat for a stone tool or two farmers exchanged corn for carrots. In short, people conducted business in a personal capacity.

With the development of science and technology, the old concept of business done on one's private capacity became a problem: How would a rich man take upon himself the liabilities (负债) associated with a large scale (大规模) rail track laying (轨道铺设) company? How would he risk all his fortune by sending trade ships to India? In short, business became a proposition (代名词) of high risk, high investment, and high return.

The idea and tool of a company were created by a couple of lords in 1896 in the British House of Lords (英国上议院) and a bootmaker named Solomon. They proposed the concept of a fictitious (虚构的) identity that could be created by individuals. So, they could get into business and succeed or fail independently from its owners. The new idea soon spread across continental Europe and America and became what we know today as a company. In a limited liability (有限责任) company, a man could do business through an independent legal identity (合法身份). The owners would have a right to the assets and rights to the management of the company.

Through the following ages, there is little change in these basic principles. Nowadays, there are many types of companies in different countries, but the same basic concepts remain.

## Task 1

Read the above passage and answer the following questions.

1. Why did people exchange things in the earliest days?
2. How did the concept of company come into being?

## Task 2

Think about the following questions and discuss in small groups.

1. What do you need to do when meeting new clients?
2. What will you do after exchanging the contact information with clients?

# Warm-up

## Task

The item "company" is familiar to us. Suppose you have an opportunity to start a company—what kind of companies would you like to choose? What preparations should you make? Could you name a company? Discuss with your team members and fill in the blanks below. Then give a presentation in your class.

| Names of Company | Types of Company | Preparations |
| --- | --- | --- |
|  |  |  |
|  |  |  |
|  |  |  |
|  |  |  |

Unit 2 | Introducing Companies 33

# Business Communication

## Part Ⅰ Introduce Business Scope

In this part, you will hear a business conversation between two native speakers. They introduce their business scope. This part consists of 3 activities. After each listening task, some useful language points will be discussed and you might use them in the following speaking task.

### Words and Expressions

| | | | |
|---|---|---|---|
| be engaged (in/on sth.) | | | to be busy doing sth. 忙于；从事于 |
| scope | /skəʊp/ | n. | The scope of an activity, topic, or piece of work is the whole area which it deals with or includes. 范围 |
| appliance | /əˈplaɪəns/ | n. | a device or machine in your home that you use to do a job such as cleaning or cooking 家用电器 |

### Activity 1　Extensive Listening

Listen to the conversation and decide whether the following statements are true (T) or false (F).

1. The man is generally engaged in export.　　　　　　　　　　　　　(　　)
2. The man mainly trades with American firms.　　　　　　　　　　　(　　)
3. Toys and stationeries are included in his business scope.　　　　　　(　　)

### Activity 2　Intensive Listening

#### Task 1 ▶

Listen to the conversation again and answer the following questions.

1. What firms does the man trade with?
2. Do you know the man's business scope?
3. Does the man generally work on import?

## Task 2

Listen to the conversation again and fill in the blanks with no more than three words.

A: What kind of trade are you generally in?

B: We _____ export.

A: What countries do you _____?

B: We mainly trade with Japanese firms.

A: What's your _____?

B: Our business scope includes clothes, stationeries, toys, household electric appliances and _____.

## Activity 3  Speaking

### Language Bank

When introducing your company to a new client for the first time, you might need to introduce your business scope for future cooperation. Here are some common expressions you might use.

**Asking for business scope:**

What kind of trade are you generally in?

What countries do you trade with?

What's your business scope?

Could you introduce your business scope?

**Introducing business scope:**

We are engaged in export/import…

We mainly trade with…

Our business scope includes…

Use the expressions above. Create your own business conversation and practice it with your partner.

### Situation

Role No. 1  You're the sales manager and meet the boss of ×××Company for the first time.

Role No. 2  You're the boss of ×××Company and you want to ask for the business scope.

Unit 2 | Introducing Companies    35

# Part II  Introduce Employees

In this part, you will hear a business conversation between two native speakers. They introduce the workforce of a company. This part consists of 3 activities. After each listening task, some useful language points will be discussed and you might use them in the following speaking task.

### Words and Expressions

| louver | /ˈluːvə(r)/ | n. | a window blind or shutter with horizontal slats that are angled to admit light and air, but to keep out rain and direct sunshine 百叶窗 |
| Frankfurt | /ˈfræŋkfət/ | n. | a city in Germany 法兰克福（德国） |

## Activity 1  Extensive Listening

Listen to the conversation and decide whether the following statements are true (T) or false (F).

1. The speakers are talking about different departments in the company.  (    )
2. The company has offices all over the world.  (    )
3. The company has the most employees in Frankfurt.  (    )

## Activity 2  Intensive Listening

### Task 1 ▶

Listen to the conversation again and answer the following questions.

1. How many employees are there in Frankfurt?
2. Does this company have employees in France?
3. How many employees work out of Germany?

### Task 2

Listen to the conversation again and fill in the blanks with no more than three words.

A: How many _____ do you have?

B: In Frankfurt, we have about _____ employees. _____ about another 35 in Stockstadt (施托克施塔特) who are doing the louver window business. And then we have about _____ 15 people in our _____ in Japan… in Tokyo, in China, in the United States and in _____.

### Activity 3  Speaking

## Language Bank

When you are introducing your company, your clients might be interested in the workforce of your company. Here are some common expressions that might help you.

**Asking for information about employees:**

How many employees do you have?

How many employees are there in… (company/city/office)?

How many people work in… (company/city/office)?

**Describing employees:**

In… (company/city/office), we have about… (number) employees.

There are about… (number) employees in… (company/city/office).

Use the expressions above. Create your own business conversation and practice it with your partner.

### Situation

**Role No. 1** You're talking with your business partner for further cooperation, and you are very interested in the workforce of his company.

**Role No. 2** You are the CEO of ××× Company and would like to introduce your company to your business partner.

# Part III  Introduce Company History

Anthony Rowe is a printer based in the South of England. Daren Armstrong works in the sales department of the company. Let us look at how he introduces the history of Anthony Rowe.

## Words and Expressions

| printer | /ˈprɪntə(r)/ | n. | a person or company whose job is printing things such as books 印刷工；印刷公司 |
| primarily | /ˈpraɪmərəli/ | ad. | what is mainly true in a particular situation 主要地 |
| niche | /nɪtʃ/ | n. | A niche in the market is a specific area of marketing which has its own particular requirements, customers and products. (有特定的要求、顾客群和产品的) 专营市场 |
| facility | /fəˈsɪləti/ | n. | buildings, pieces of equipment, or services that are provided for a particular purpose 设施，设备 |

### Activity 1  Extensive Watching

Watch a short video and answer the following questions.

1. What is the video mainly about?
2. Who started Antony Rowe?
3. Does Antony Rowe have book printing facilities in China?

## Activity 2  Intensive Watching

### Task 1

Watch the video again and choose the correct answers.

1. When was Antony Rowe purchased by his CPI?
   A. 6 years ago.   B. 30 years ago.
   C. 7 years ago.   D. 4 years ago.

2. How many book printing facilities are there in France?
   A. 1.   B. 2.
   C. 3.   D. 7.

### Task 2

Watch the video again and fill in the blanks.

A: Tell us about the _____ of Antony Rowe.

B: Antony Rowe was _____ by Antony Rowe himself. Around 30 years ago, he started the company because primarily there was a niche in the market for what is short run… short run produced books. Antony Rowe was _____ by his CPI six years ago. And we have since grown to be _____ of the… the UK side of that group. And CPI is… is European based. Its _____ are in Paris. We have seven printing facilities… book printing facilities in France. We have three _____ facilities in Germany, two in the Netherlands (荷兰), one in the Czech Republic (捷克共和国), one in Spain and seven in the UK. So Antony Rowe is part of… of seven companies within the UK.

## Activity 3  Speaking

## Language Bank

If you want to introduce the history of your company, you can use some common expressions as follows.

### Introducing company history:

Our company was started/established/founded/set up in… (year)/… (number) years ago.

Around… (number) years ago, ×××(name)/he started the company/××× Company.

××× Company has a history of…

### Introducing headquarters/head offices:

××× Company is headquartered/based in… (place).

The headquarters/head offices of… (company) are in… (place).

Our head offices are (located) in… (place).

We are based in… (place).

### Introducing company development:

We have since grown to be a major part of…

Our company had developed into…

Antony Rowe was purchased by his CPI six years ago.

Antony Rowe is part of seven companies within the UK.

### Introducing company performance:

We are the market leaders in three countries.

We have expanded our operations.

Our company has grown by one-third this year.

We make annual profits of $1 million.

Our turnover is in excess of $2 million.

◉ Task 1 ▸

Use the expressions you've just learned as prompts and watch the video again. Then practice the conversation with your partner.

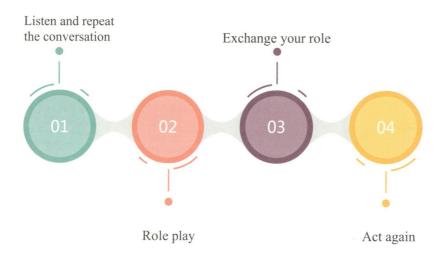

01 Listen and repeat the conversation
02 Role play
03 Exchange your role
04 Act again

◉ Task 2 ▸

Use the expressions above. Create your own business conversation and practice it with your group members.

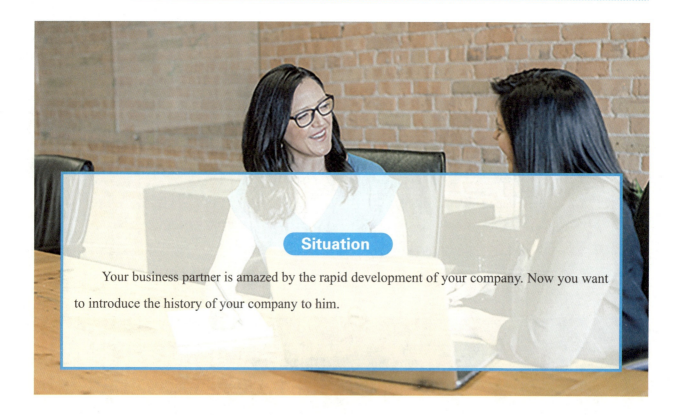

**Situation**

Your business partner is amazed by the rapid development of your company. Now you want to introduce the history of your company to him.

# Part IV  Introduce Departments

In this part, you will watch a short video about company departments. This part consists of 3 tasks. After each watching and listening task, some useful language points will be discussed and you might use them in the following speaking task.

## Words and Expressions

| | | | |
|---|---|---|---|
| department | /dɪˈpɑːtmənt/ | n. | one of the sections in an organization such as a government, business, or university（政府、企业等机构的）部门 |
| adequate | /ˈædɪkwət/ | a. | If something is adequate, there is enough of it or it is good enough to be used or accepted. 足够的 |
| graphic | /ˈɡræfɪk/ | a. | to be concerned with drawing or pictures, especially in publishing, industry, or computing 绘图的；图画的 |
| digital | /ˈdɪdʒɪtl/ | a. | Digital systems record or transmit information in the form of thousands of very small signals. 数码的 |
| dispatch | /dɪˈspætʃ/ | n. | the act of sending off something 派遣，发送 |

### Activity 1  Extensive Watching

Watch a short video and answer the following questions.

1. What is Anthony Rowe?
2. How many departments does Anthony Rowe have?
3. Are there many printing departments in Anthony Rowe?

### Activity 2  Intensive Watching

**Task 1**

Watch the video again and choose the correct answers.

1. What is the first department?
   A. Customer service department.
   B. Pre-production department.
   C. Graphic printing department.
   D. Dispatch department.

2. Which department does Daren Armstrong work in?
   A. Printing department.
   B. Finance estimating department.
   C. Dispatch department.
   D. Sales department.

## Task 2

Watch the video again and fill in the blanks.

A: Anthony Rowe is a printer _____ the South of England. Daren Armstrong works in the _____ of the company. How many departments does Anthony Rowe have?

B: On this site, we have 14 departments. The first department we have is _____, that's _____ pre-production or pre-press, which is to make sure that what the customer supplies us is of adequate use for further _____. We have a number of _____, like the graphic printing which is inked on paper, a digital printing which is I suppose best described as large photocopies, as well as _____. Then we also have a dispatch department, goods-in department, finance estimating (财务评估) and sales.

## Activity 3  Speaking

### Language Bank

When introducing your company's departments, you can use some common expressions as follows.

**Asking for departments information:**

How many departments does… (company) have?
Could you introduce your departments?
What departments does… (company) have?

**Describing departments:**

We have… (number) departments.
The first department we have is…
××× department is to make sure that…
We have a number of departments like…

Unit 2 | Introducing Companies

## Task 1

Use the expressions you've just learned to complete the following conversation. Then practice it with your partner.

Anna: Hi, Tom. I am curious about your company. _____?

Tom: Of course. What are you most interested in? Company history or departments?

Anna: Well, departments. _____ does your company have?

Tom: On this site, _____, each with its own director. _____ sales department. This department is responsible for the sale of products. _____ research and development department which plays an important role in the life cycle (生命周期) of a product. _____ human resources department and finance department.

## Task 2

Use the expressions above. Create your own business conversation and practice it with your group members.

**Situation**

You're in a business meeting and want to introduce your company departments to your business partners.

# Project-based Task

## Objectives

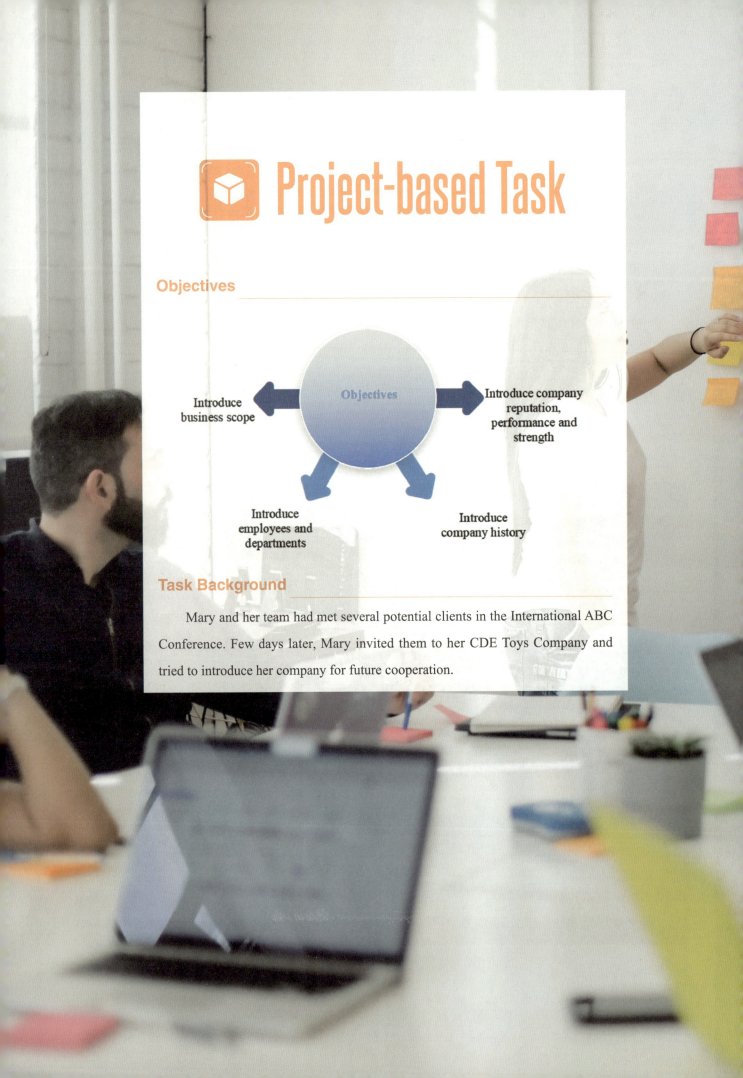

## Task Background

Mary and her team had met several potential clients in the International ABC Conference. Few days later, Mary invited them to her CDE Toys Company and tried to introduce her company for future cooperation.

## Procedures

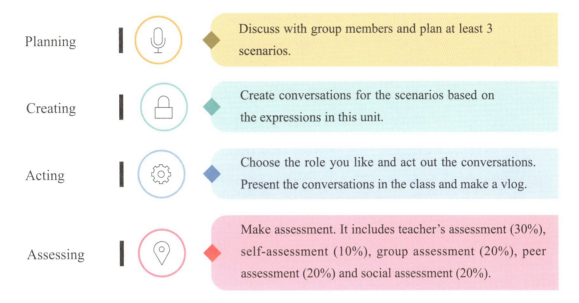

Planning — Discuss with group members and plan at least 3 scenarios.

Creating — Create conversations for the scenarios based on the expressions in this unit.

Acting — Choose the role you like and act out the conversations. Present the conversations in the class and make a vlog.

Assessing — Make assessment. It includes teacher's assessment (30%), self-assessment (10%), group assessment (20%), peer assessment (20%) and social assessment (20%).

## Possible Scenarios

### Scenario 1

Mary has invited the new clients she met at the International ABC Conference to her company. She shows them around the company. The new clients are very interested in CDE Toys Company and want to know more about it. So, firstly, Mary would like to introduce the business scope.

Role No. 1  Mary: Introduce the business scope of CDE Toys Company…

Role No. 2  Mary's assistant: Prepare some brochures…

Role No. 3  Manager of ××× Company

Role No. 4  CEO of ××× Company

…

## Scenario 2

After introducing the business scope, Mary would also like to introduce her teammates and employees who are so diligent and helpful. They move to different departments.

Role No. 1  Mary: Introduce the total number of the employees and several departments…

Role No. 2  Manager of sales department: Greet other people and introduce herself…

Role No. 3  Manager of R&D department: Greet other people and introduce himself…

Role No. 4  CEO of ××× Company: Ask questions about career development of employees…

Role No. 5  Manager of ××× Company: Ask questions about future plan for departments…

…

## Scenario 3

The new clients are astonished at the rapid development of CDE Toys Company. They want to know more about the history of the company. So, they arrive at the conference room and Mary is going to make a presentation about the company history, reputation and strength to promote the new products.

Role No. 1  Mary: Make a presentation about the company history, reputation and strength to promote the new products…

Role No. 2  Mary's assistant: Show the models of the new toys…

Role No. 3  Manager of ××× Company: Ask information about the new products…

Role No. 4  CEO of ××× Company: Ask information about the awards the company won this year…

…

Requirements:

- All group members are required to take part in the project.
- Use the expressions you have learned in this unit as many as possible.

# Self-assessment Checklist

Now, it's time for you to review your performance after learning this unit. Carry out a self-assessment by checking the following table.

| Items | | Ratings | | | |
|---|---|---|---|---|---|
| | | A | B | C | D |
| Listening Skills | I can recognize the expressions about locations and directions. | | | | |
| | I can understand the basic information of a company. | | | | |
| | I can understand the business scope of a company. | | | | |
| | I can catch the information about employees. | | | | |
| | I can understand the information about company history. | | | | |
| | I can understand the information about company headquarters and branches. | | | | |
| | I can understand the information about company development and performance. | | | | |
| | I can catch the information about departments. | | | | |
| Speaking Skills | I can give the information about locations and directions. | | | | |
| | I can describe the basic information of a company. | | | | |
| | I can introduce the business scope of a company. | | | | |
| | I can introduce basic information of employees. | | | | |
| | I can describe company history. | | | | |
| | I can introduce company headquarters and branches. | | | | |
| | I can introduce company development and performance. | | | | |
| | I can catch the information about departments. | | | | |
| Professional Skills | I can introduce the business scope of my company to business partners. | | | | |
| | I can introduce basic information of employees and departments to business partners. | | | | |
| | I can talk about company history, headquarters and branches, development and performance to attract business partners. | | | | |
| | I can make a presentation with PPT to introduce our company. | | | | |

A: Basically agree

B: Agree

C: Strongly agree

D: Disagree

# Unit 3
## Attending Meetings

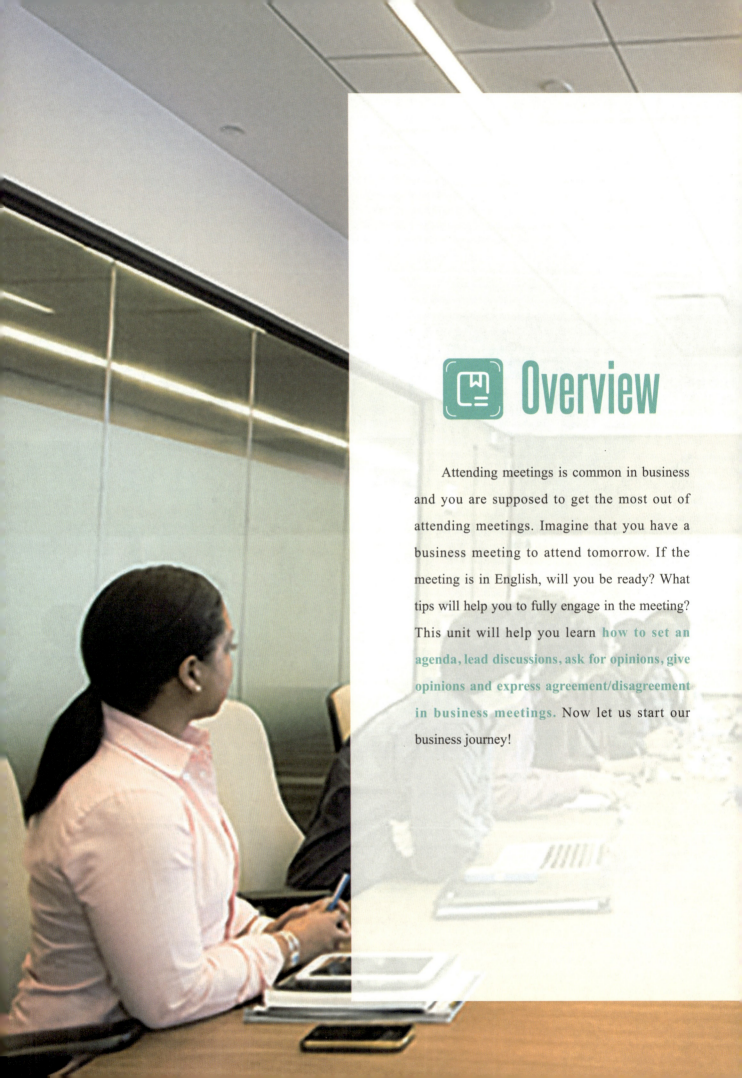

# Overview

Attending meetings is common in business and you are supposed to get the most out of attending meetings. Imagine that you have a business meeting to attend tomorrow. If the meeting is in English, will you be ready? What tips will help you to fully engage in the meeting? This unit will help you learn **how to set an agenda, lead discussions, ask for opinions, give opinions and express agreement/disagreement in business meetings.** Now let us start our business journey!

# Listening Strategies

## Understanding Instructions

It is important for us to understand the instructions, particularly when we carry out a program. In this part, we are going to learn how to ask for and give instructions as well as check understanding in English. Here we focus on the tips of giving instructions.

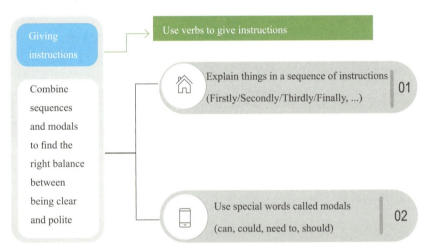

Here are some typical expressions to ask for and give instructions as well as check understanding.

Unit 3 | Attending Meetings

## Ask for Instructions

1. Can you show me how to…?
2. Do you know how to…?
3. How do I (go about)…?
4. What do you suggest?
5. What is the first step?
6. What is the best way to…?

## Give Instructions

1. Firstly/To begin with/To start out, you need to make an appointment.
2. Secondly, arrange for the meeting.
3. Next, I'd like you to make a suggestion.
4. Finally/In the end, don't forget to discuss with your team members.

## Check Understanding

1. Do you understand?
2. Is everyone clear about what to do now?
3. Any questions about what you need to do?

### Task ▶

Listen to the conversation and fill in the blanks. You can try to draw a flow chart to help you get the instructions.

### 🔊 Conversation 1

Mary: Excuse me! _____ me with this?

Lin: Yep. _____, try turning the computer on.

Mary: OK, I did that… What is the _____?

Lin: Then open this document and _____.

Mary: OK, finished.

Lin: Now _____ on that icon.

Mary: Fantastic. I get it! Thanks, Lin.

Lin: My pleasure.

## Conversation 2

Harry: Amy, I am very interested in Chinese tea. _____ make it?

Amy: It is simple. Let me tell you. First, _____ some water. While you are waiting the water to boil, _____ some tea leaves _____ a tea pot.

Harry: OK. Then?

Amy: Then pour the boiling water into the tea pot and wait a few minutes _____.

Harry: That's it! Thanks.

## Conversation 3

Jane: Hi, Tom. _____ how to cook this soup? It smells good.

Tom: Of course. _____, you _____ cut the chicken into small pieces and boil some water in a pot.

Jane: Yep. I got it. _____?

Tom: When the water starts to boil, put the chicken in it.

Jane: It sounds great.

Tom: _____ to add some fresh vegetables like carrots, corn and potatoes to improve the taste.

Jane: Is that all for the soup?

Tom: Not yet. _____ to add some pepper and salt.

Jane: Yes! Thank you for your recipe (菜谱) and you _____.

Tom: You're welcome. I hope you can enjoy it.

# Cultural Background

Most of us attend business meetings day in and day out. The best ideas come when great minds come together. Most meetings take place either to communicate something or to discuss a topic and reach agreement on strategy-making. There is no doubt that the chairperson's skills to run a meeting are essential (基本的). Actually, our participation as attendees is also crucial to the meeting's success. Here are some tips for attendees to get the most out of business meetings.

**Be prepared**

When you are invited to attend a business meeting, read the agenda first. The agenda will outline the objective and important items of the meeting so you know how to prepare accordingly. This can help you to best absorb (理解, 吸收) all of the new information you obtain in the meeting.

**Take notes**

Meetings often contain key information and tasks that you need to remember in the future. You can either keep notes or record the meeting to refresh yourself, but always make sure recording is okay with the meeting's host. Taking notes also keeps your mind focused on the information instead of wandering to other things.

**Ask questions**

If you have a real question or feedback that would be valuable to the meeting, don't hesitate to share. If you don't understand a specific part of the meeting, always speak up. Otherwise, you're only wasting your time.

**Follow up**

You might have questions after a meeting or be tasked with some action items. When given specific responsibilities to carry out the tasks, be sure to complete those things within the time frame. And if you still have some questions, seek clarification or check understanding.

In short, before attending a meeting, be prepared. Be willing to participate and unafraid to ask the difficult questions. Having active attendees makes meetings run much more smoothly and effectively.

## Task 1

Read the above passage and answer the following questions.

1. What is the main idea of the above passage?
2. What are the tips introduced in the above passage?

## Task 2

Think about the following questions and discuss in small groups.

1. What should you consider about when taking notes in meetings?
2. What will you do if you cannot follow up what's being discussed in the meeting?

# Warm-up

## Task

When you saw the following cloud picture, what's the first word that comes into your eyes? Maybe the word "agree" or "disagree". Now let us write down the words we can see in the cloud picture and predict (猜测) what phrases and expressions we will learn about business meeting in this unit. After finishing this task, share your ideas with your classmates.

Unit 3 | Attending Meetings  57

## Part I  Set an Agenda

An office meeting has been scheduled, but Paul is running late. He's asked Anna to take charge and start the meeting without him. Anna has to learn how to start a meeting. This part consists of 3 activities. After each listening task, some useful language points will be discussed and you might use them in the following speaking task.

| Words and Expressions | | | |
|---|---|---|---|
| stock | /stɒk/ | n. | A company's stock is the amount of money which the company has through selling shares. （公司的）股票价值 |
| item | /ˈaɪtəm/ | n. | one of a list of things for someone to do, deal with, or talk about 项目 |
| wrap up | | | If you wrap up something such as a job or an agreement, you complete it in a satisfactory way. 圆满完成（工作）；达成（协议） |

### Activity 1  Extensive Listening

Listen to the conversation and decide whether the following statements are true (T) or false (F).

1. The speaker helps Paul to start the meeting. (　　)
2. There are five items on the agenda today. (　　)
3. They will discuss a team-building activity in the meeting. (　　)

## Activity 2  Intensive Listening

### Task 1

Listen to the conversation again and answer the following questions.

1. How many items are there on the agenda today?
2. Does Paul attend the meeting on time?
3. What is the first item on the agenda?

### Task 2

Listen to the conversation again and fill in the blanks with no more than three words.

(The meeting starts)

Anna:  Thank you… thank you for _____. Paul will be here soon, but he asked me to start the meeting. There are (counting) one, two, three, four items on the _____ today. Firstly, the stock management systems. Secondly, plans for a _____ (collective groan). After that, the color of our new apples and finally any other business, before we can _____.

Paul:  (arriving) Oh golly gosh, there you are, here I am, good. Hello, everyone. Sorry, I'm late.

Anna:  I'd just _____.

Paul:  Great. Remind me what the first _____ on the agenda is.

## Activity 3  Speaking

### Language Bank

When starting a meeting, you might need to welcome the attendees and introduce the agenda. Here are some common expressions you might use.

**Welcoming the attendees:**

Thank you for coming. Now let us get down to the business.
I'd like to welcome you all here today. Perhaps we can make a start.
Thanks everyone and welcome today's meeting. Let's begin.

**Introducing the agenda:**

There are… (number) items on the agenda today.

Unit 3 | Attending Meetings 59

Firstly, … Secondly, … After that, … and finally…

The first item/topic on the agenda is…

Have you all received a copy of the agenda today?

Use the expressions above. Create your own business conversation and practice it with your partner.

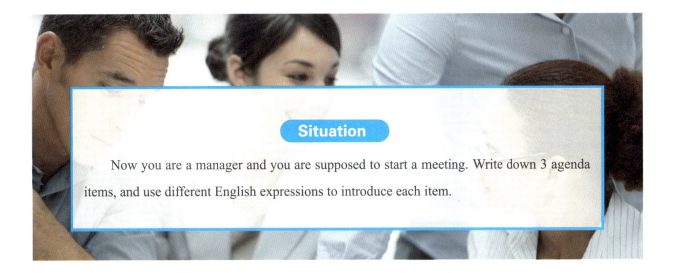

**Situation**

Now you are a manager and you are supposed to start a meeting. Write down 3 agenda items, and use different English expressions to introduce each item.

## Part II  Lead Discussions and Ask for Opinions

In this part, you will hear a business conversation in a meeting where the chairman tries to lead discussions and ask for opinions. This part consists of 3 activities. After each listening task, some useful language points will be discussed and you might use them in the following speaking task.

| Words and Expressions | | | |
|---|---|---|---|
| budget | /ˈbʌdʒɪt/ | n. | The budget for something is the amount of money that a person, organization, or country has available to spend on it. 预算 |
| boost | /buːst/ | v. | If one thing boosts another, it causes it to increase, improve, or be more successful. 促进 |
| allocate | /ˈæləkeɪt/ | v. | If one item or share of something is allocated to a particular person or for a particular purpose, it is given to that person or used for that purpose. 分配 |
| priority | /praɪˈɒrətɪ/ | n. | If something is a priority, it is the most important thing you have to do or deal with, or must be done or dealt with before everything else you have to do. 优先处理的事 |

## Activity 1    Extensive Listening

Listen to the conversation and decide whether the following statements are true (T) or false (F).

1. The sales have been increasing recently.    (    )
2. The speaker asked Jamie and Lynn to give opinions.    (    )
3. They should decide how to use this advertising money.    (    )

## Activity 2    Intensive Listening

### Task 1

Listen to the conversation again and answer the following questions.

1. What has been done to boost sales?
2. What is the first question for the meeting?
3. What do they need to decide?

### Task 2

Listen to the conversation again and fill in the blanks with no more than three words.

A: We all know that _____ have been dropping, so management has decided to increase the _____ to boost sales. So, we _____ how to allocate this advertising money. The first _____ is media. What should our priority be: TV, movies, print, billboards or public transport? I'd like to get all your _____. Let's _____ you, Jamie. What do you think? (Where should we advertise?)

(Some time later)

A: Okay, we now need to discuss the _____. Lynn, what's your opinion on the timing? When do you think we should begin the advertising campaign?

Unit 3 | Attending Meetings

## Activity 3  Speaking

### Language Bank

Leading discussions and asking for opinions play an important part in the success of meeting. Here are some common expressions that might help you.

**Leading discussions:**

We all know that… (background), so…

The first question is…

Okay, we now need to discuss…

**Asking for opinions:**

I'd like to get all your opinions.

Let's start with you, ××× (name). What do you think?

What's your opinion on…?

When do you think we should…?

Where should we advertise?

What should our priority be?

Use the expressions above. Create your own business conversation and practice it with your partner.

### Situation

Now you are the manager of ××× Company and you are supposed to chair a meeting to discuss the marketing strategy. Try to lead discussions and ask for opinions.

# Part III  Give Opinions

A marketing meeting is carried out to discuss the marketing strategy and come up with ideas for the next campaign. All the members have their own opinions. Watch the video and pay attention to how they give opinions. After each watching and listening task, some useful language points will be discussed and you might use them in the following speaking task.

### Words and Expressions

| | | | |
|---|---|---|---|
| review | /rɪˈvjuː/ | v. | If you review a situation or system, you consider it carefully to see what is wrong with it or how it could be improved. 审裁; 审度 |
| strategy | /ˈstrætədʒɪ/ | n. | a general plan or set of plans intended to achieve something, especially over a long period 策略 |
| target | /ˈtɑːgɪt/ | v. | If you target a particular group of people, you try to appeal to those people or affect them. 以（某特定人群）为目标; 针对 |
| traditional | /trəˈdɪʃənl/ | a. | Traditional customs, beliefs, or methods are ones that have existed for a long time without changing. 传统的 |
| supplement | /ˈsʌplɪmənt/ | n. | a separate part of a magazine or newspaper, often dealing with a particular topic（报纸或杂志的）增刊 |
| chic | /ʃiːk/ | a. | something or someone that is chic is fashionable and sophisticated 时髦且有品位的 |
| boutique | /buːˈtiːk/ | n. | a small shop that sells fashionable clothes, shoes, or jewelry 时尚精品小店 |
| minutes | /ˈmɪnɪts/ | n. | The minutes of a meeting are the written records of the things that are discussed or decided at it. 会议记录 |

### Activity 1  Extensive Watching

Watch a short video and answer the following questions.

1. What is the object of this meeting?
2. Do these speakers have a heated discussion?
3. Do these speakers finish the discussion today? How do you know?

Unit 3 | Attending Meetings  63

## Activity 2  Intensive Watching

### Task 1

Watch the video again and choose the correct answers.

1. According to Sally, which age range of women is over-focused in their current strategy?
   A. 25-35.              B. 30-45.
   C. 45-50.              D. 55-65.
2. Who will they consider hiring?
   A. A project manager.        B. An advertising designer.
   C. A sales manager.          D. A social media manager.

### Task 2

Watch the video again and fill in the blanks.

Chairwoman: So, what can we do to reach this target? Allen, do you have any _____?

Allen: _____ using social media? Our advertising is mainly based around traditional media such as print and television. Nobody under 25 reads newspapers anymore.

Sally: _____ about that. Fashion magazines and supplements _____ in our overall marketing mix (营销组合).

Allen: Yes. But we need to be using Twitter and Facebook too, if we want to increase our market share among Millennials.

Kevin: Can I make a suggestion?

Chairwoman: Of course, Kevin.

Kevin: _____ we hire a social media manager? Someone who could _____ potential customers and promote the chic boutique brand online.

Chairwoman: That's a good idea! It's certainly something we should consider. I'll _____ at next week's board meeting.

### Activity 3 — Speaking

## Language Bank

When discussing in a meeting, you can use some common expressions as follows.

**Giving opinions:**

What about using social media?

Can I make a suggestion?

Why don't we hire a social media manager?

But we need to be using Twitter and Facebook too…

We have to/ought to improve the way we collect and record sales data.

**Agreeing with opinions:**

I agree with…

That's a good idea! It's certainly something we should consider.

Let's go with this idea.

**Asking questions:**

So, what can we do to reach this target?

How…?

Excuse me/Sorry to interrupt, does this mean…?

**Concluding the meeting:**

Right, I think we've covered everything.

OK, that's all for today's meeting. Are there any questions before we finish?

And we can start thinking about the agenda for the next meeting. Thank you everyone!

Unit 3 | Attending Meetings 65

## Task 1 ▶

Role play. Use the expressions you've just learned as prompts and watch the video again. Then practice beginning a meeting with your partner.

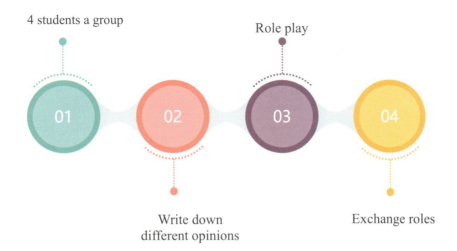

01 — 4 students a group
02 — Write down different opinions
03 — Role play
04 — Exchange roles

## Task 2 ▶

Use the expressions above. Create your own business conversation and practice it with your group members.

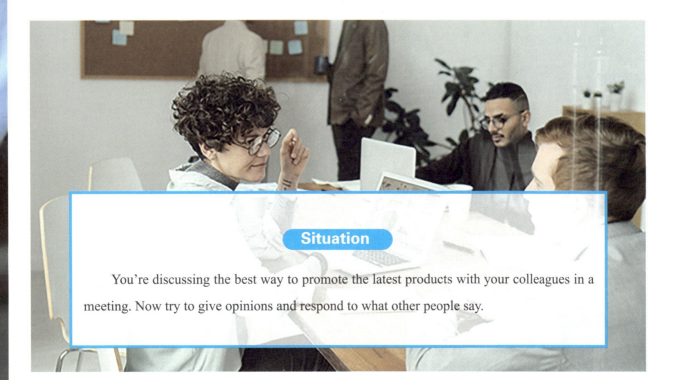

**Situation**

You're discussing the best way to promote the latest products with your colleagues in a meeting. Now try to give opinions and respond to what other people say.

# Part IV  Disagree Opinions

Tom, Anna and Denise get together to share their ideas about Tip Top Trading's upcoming launch, but their opinions differ. Anna's ideas are met with some negative (否定的) comments and she has to learn how to disagree with the other's viewpoint in a confident but polite manner. This part consists of 3 tasks. After each watching and listening task, some useful language points will be discussed and you might use them in the following speaking task.

## Words and Expressions

| | | | |
|---|---|---|---|
| desperate | /ˈdespərət/ | a. | If you are desperate for something or desperate to do something, you want or need it very much indeed. 极度渴望的 |
| point | /pɔɪnt/ | n. | something that someone has said or written 看法 |
| get rid of | | | to do away with 去除，摆脱，处理掉 |

### Activity 1  Extensive Watching

Watch a short video and answer the following questions.

1. How many speakers took part in this meeting?
2. Did these speakers have the same opinion?
3. Did these speakers get a final decision?

### Activity 2  Intensive Watching

#### Task 1

Watch the video again and choose the correct answers.

1. What is the discount for all regular clients for this month at last?
   A. 5%.　　　　B. 10%.　　　　C. 15%.　　　　D. 20%.
2. Who will make a presentation?
   A. Tom.　　　　B. Denise.　　　　C. Anna.　　　　D. Paul.

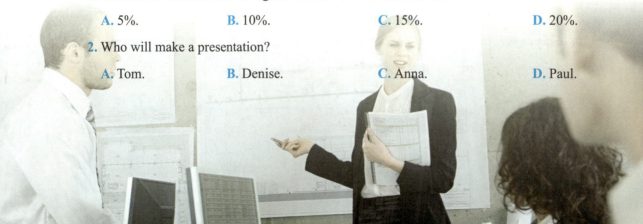

Unit 3 | Attending Meetings

### Task 2

Watch the video again and fill in the blanks.

Anna: OK. Well, _____ about that. I think it will improve our sales of lemons and make our clients happy. Happy clients will come back to buy more.

Paul: Yes, that's a _____, Annabe… Anna.

Tom: But 20% is a lot—maybe 5% would be better.

Anna: But if we're going to _____, we should make it so good that everyone will say yes!

Denise: But people might think there's something _____ with our lemons and that we're desperate to get rid of them.

Anna: I see your point, but, if we explain this is just a special offer for special clients, they'll understand.

Paul: I like that idea. Good. 20% off for all regular _____ just for this month. Anna, you'll be making the presentation to Citrus Ventures, so make sure you _____ that offer.

Anna: Yes.

Paul: Right, next, what photos do we have of the lemons?

## Activity 3  Speaking

### Language Bank

When discussing in a meeting, you can use some common expressions as follows.

**Disagreeing opinions:**

I'm not so sure about that…

I see your point, but actually I think…

But…

Maybe… would be better.

**Commenting:**

Yes, that's a good point.

I like that idea. Good.

I get your point.

**Moving forwards:**

Right, next, what photos do we have…?

So, if there's nothing else we need to discuss, let us move on to the next item.

### Task 1

Pair work. Use the expressions you've just learned to complete the following conversation. Then practice it with your partner.

A: OK. Well, _____. I think it will improve our sales of apples and make our clients happy.

B: Yes, _____.

C: But 30% is a lot—maybe 10% _____.

A: _____ make a special offer, we should make it so attractive that everyone will say yes!

D: _____ our apples are not good and we're desperate to get rid of them.

A: _____, but, if we explain this is just a special offer for special clients, they'll understand.

B: Great. So, we decide to give 30% off for all regular clients just for this week. And _____.

### Task 2

Use the expressions above. Create your own business conversation and practice it with your group members.

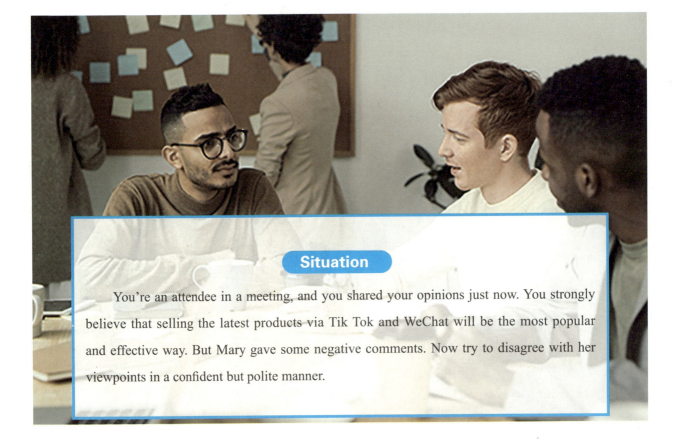

**Situation**

You're an attendee in a meeting, and you shared your opinions just now. You strongly believe that selling the latest products via Tik Tok and WeChat will be the most popular and effective way. But Mary gave some negative comments. Now try to disagree with her viewpoints in a confident but polite manner.

# Project-based Task

## Objectives

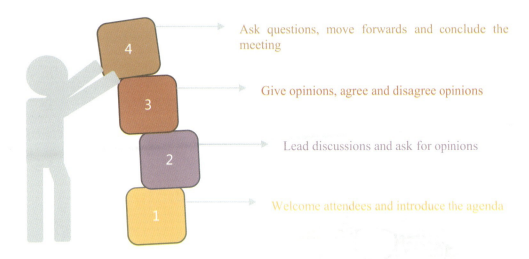

4 — Ask questions, move forwards and conclude the meeting

3 — Give opinions, agree and disagree opinions

2 — Lead discussions and ask for opinions

1 — Welcome attendees and introduce the agenda

## Task Background

A formal meeting is scheduled in ABC Company to discuss the marketing strategy and come up with valuable ideas for the next campaign. All the members attend the meeting and share different opinions. They have a heated discussion.

## Procedures

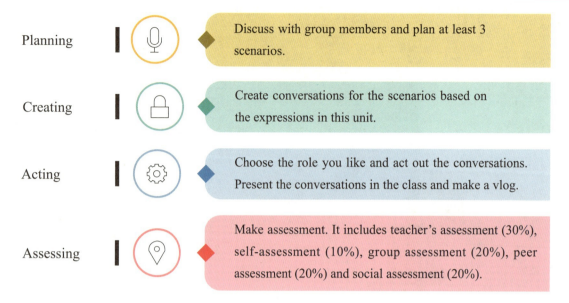

Planning — Discuss with group members and plan at least 3 scenarios.

Creating — Create conversations for the scenarios based on the expressions in this unit.

Acting — Choose the role you like and act out the conversations. Present the conversations in the class and make a vlog.

Assessing — Make assessment. It includes teacher's assessment (30%), self-assessment (10%), group assessment (20%), peer assessment (20%) and social assessment (20%).

## Possible Scenarios

### Scenario 1

Mary, CEO of ABC Toys Company, chairs a marketing meeting at the No. 1 Conference Room today. The objective of the meeting is to discuss the marketing strategy and come up with valuable ideas for the next campaign. All the employees attend the meeting and share different opinions. At first, Mary should set an agenda to introduce the important items.

Role No. 1  Mary: Thank all the members for attending and introduce the meeting agenda.

Role No. 2  Tom: Take minutes.

Role No. 3  Emily: Take notes.

…

### Scenario 2

After setting the agenda, Mary leads the discussion of item 1 and asks several attendees to make reports on last month's sales. Then, Mary asks for all the attendees' opinions after the reports.

Role No. 1  Mary: Introduce the details of item 1; ask several attendees to make reports on last month's sales; ask for all the attendees' opinions after the reports.

Role No. 2  John: Report sales of toys in Asia.

Role No. 3  Flynn: Report sales of toys in Europe.

Role No. 4  Mike: Express her opinions on the sales last month and propose the change of advertising.

…

## ◯ Scenario 3 ▶

All the attendees share different opinions and they have a heated discussion. Mary tries to keep the discussion relevant.

**Role No. 1** Mary: Keep the discussion relevant and ensure that everyone has a say in the discussion.

**Role No. 2** Mike: Express his opinions on the sales last month and propose the change of advertising.

**Role No. 3** Anna: Disagree with Mike and interrupt him.

**Role No. 4** Jane: Agree with Mike and give reasons.

**Role No. 5** Tim: Ask questions to check understanding.

…

Requirements:

- All group members are required to take part in the project.
- Use the expressions you have learned in this unit as many as possible.

# Self-assessment Checklist

Now, it's time for you to review your performance after learning this unit. Carry out a self-assessment by checking the following table.

| | Items | Ratings | | | |
|---|---|---|---|---|---|
| | | A | B | C | D |
| Listening Skills | I can recognize the expressions about instructions. | | | | |
| | I can understand welcome and introductions in business meetings. | | | | |
| | I can catch the information about the meeting agenda. | | | | |
| | I can recognize the beginning of discussions. | | | | |
| | I can understand different opinions in business meetings. | | | | |
| | I can understand the reasons for different opinions. | | | | |
| | I can tell agreement from disagreement according to opinions. | | | | |
| | I can understand the conclusions of business meetings. | | | | |
| Speaking Skills | I can ask for instructions, give instructions and check understanding. | | | | |
| | I can greet and introduce the attendees. | | | | |
| | I can lead discussions in business meetings. | | | | |
| | I can ask for opinions in business meetings. | | | | |
| | I can give opinions in business meetings. | | | | |
| | I can ask questions in business meetings. | | | | |
| | I can express my agreement and disagreement in business meetings. | | | | |
| | I can sum up and conclude the discussions/meetings. | | | | |
| Professional Skills | I can attend business meetings confidently and get prepared. | | | | |
| | I can set an agenda in business meetings. | | | | |
| | I can lead discussions and ask for opinions in business meetings. | | | | |
| | I can express my opinions, agree and disagree others' opinions in business meetings. | | | | |

A: Basically agree

B: Agree

C: Strongly agree

D: Disagree

# Unit 4

## Traveling on Business

# Overview

Traveling on business is an effective way to establish and maintain business relationships. When you begin a business travel, full preparations can ensure a smooth journey as well as a successful deal. Nowadays, with the development of modern technology, you can arrange your travel schedule with the aid of online websites or a simple call for reservation. Sometimes you can also ask your secretary or a travel agency to make arrangements. All in all, the goal of the business travel is to seek more business opportunities. Therefore, in this unit, you will learn **how to pack the luggage, arrange the trip, book a flight online and sign a contract.** Now start your business travel!

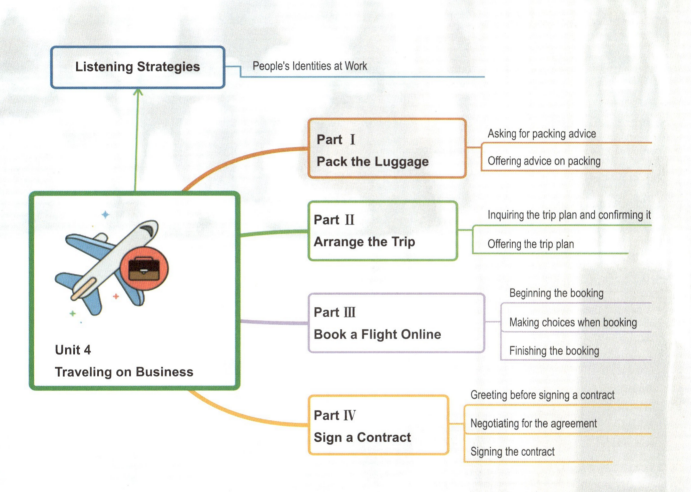

# Listening Strategies

## Understanding People's Identities

It is necessary for us to listen for the information about people's identities (身份), generally including the names, birthplaces, educational backgrounds, job titles, social positions and so on. In this part, we will focus on people's identities in the working field. The following tips can help us to understand people's identities easily. Firstly, focus on a series of WH-questions, for example, "What do you mainly do in your job?", "How do you feel about your current work?" and so on. These questions can offer us some basic facts about the speakers. Secondly, don't miss the contextual words concerning the working field, like the job titles, the conversational environment or the typical speaking patterns, because these words can give us a hint about people's current working situation and status (状态). Lastly, pay attention to people's intonations and tones (语音语调), happy or sad, energetic or exhausted, nervous or relaxed. From these implicit (隐藏的) codes we can infer the explicit (明显的) messages about the speaker's feelings, attitudes or preferences about the work.

Here are some typical expressions to show people's identities at work.

### People's Identities at Work

1. I am a marketing manager at ××× Company.
2. I work as a sales associate (销售助理) in City Insurance.
3. I take care of all the scheduling (安排).
4. I follow up customers to make sure they're satisfied with our service.
5. We're getting ready for a trade show.
6. Most of my day is spent on calling clients and handling orders.
7. I put a lot of time into writing reports.

## Task

Listen to the conversations and fill in the blanks.

### Conversation 1

A: Let's get started. Tell me a bit about your _____ background.

B: Well, I graduated from City College. My _____ is office management.

A: So, tell me, can you _____ any foreign languages?

B: Yes, I'm pretty good at English. I have _____ CET-4.

A: I see, and do you know any other language?

B: No, I can't.

### Conversation 2

A: You look so tired today.

B: Oh, yes.

A: Let's take a coffee _____, shall we?

B: Sorry. I can't.

A: Why are you so busy?

B: Well, I have got to _____.

A: You can't stay _____ forever.

B: I know. But I _____ finish it this morning.

A: Anyway, I think you do _____ to take a break.

B: Thanks for your advice.

### Conversation 3

A: Why do you want to work with our _____?

B: I want to get a more challenging job.

A: How about your _____ job?

B: My salary is not bad. But I want to _____ of this chance.

A: Alright. How did you get to know about this job?

B: I read about it in the _____.

A: Why do you think you are _____ for the job?

B: I have five years of work _____ in this field.

A: OK. Then how much _____ do you expect from this job?

B: No less than 5,000 *yuan* per month.

A: Do you have any questions?

B: Not at the moment.

A: Right. We'll _____ you when we have made a decision.

B: Thank you for the interview.

A: You are welcome.

# Lead-in

## Cultural Background

Business travel refers to any type of geographical transportation that someone takes on behalf of the employer to perform the job duties. The business travelers should check travel advisories (公告), prepare luggage, and choose a fast-speed and convenient type of transportation. Whether you work for a large international company or a small local firm, you should adapt yourself to traveling on business. The purposes of business travel can be quite various: from attending conference to taking business training, from seeking new clients to maintaining customer relationship, from visiting a company to inspecting a factory…

According to a survey, business travel makes up a big traveling volume and contributes (做出贡献) greatly to the total domestic and international travel expenses every year. Three tips are here for your business traveling: planning ahead is always the best way to start your travel; arranging your travel by surfing the internet, or through the cooperative travel agency; and keeping an eye on your important belongings as well as personal health and security during the trip. Now, get ready for your successful business travel, you are sure to achieve a win-win situation for yourself and your businesses.

### Task 1 ▶

Read the above passage and answer the following questions.

1. What's the purpose of a business travel?
2. What are the tips for a good business travel?

### Task 2 ▶

Think about the following questions and discuss them in groups.

1. What do you need to take with you when setting off a business trip?
2. Can you book an airport ticket online? What will you do when booking a flight online?

# Warm-up

## Task

The following phrases show you something related to business travel. Which one do you like/dislike most? Discuss with your group members and state your reasons.

- meeting new clients
- packing suitcases
- taking a plane
- queuing at check-in
- having jet lag
- making flight and hotel reservations
- visiting new places
- speaking a foreign language

# Business Communication

## Part I  Pack the Luggage

In this part, you will hear a business conversation between two native speakers. They talk about packing the luggage for the business trip. This part consists of 3 activities. After each listening task, some useful language points will be discussed and you might use them in the following speaking task.

### Words and Expressions

| | | | |
|---|---|---|---|
| pack | /pæk/ | v. | to put clothes, etc. into a bag in preparation for a trip away from home 收拾（行李）；装（箱） |
| laptop | /ˈlæptɒp/ | n. | a small computer that can work with a battery and be easily carried 膝上型计算机；便携式电脑；笔记本电脑 |
| charger | /ˈtʃɑːdʒə(r)/ | n. | a device for charging a battery or battery-powered equipment 充电器 |
| carry-on | /ˈkærɪ ɒn/ | n. | a bag or suitcase suitable for taking on to an aircraft as hand luggage 手提行李，登机行李 |
| luggage | /ˈlʌɡɪdʒ/ | n. | bags, cases, etc. that contain somebody's clothes and things when they are travelling 行李 |

### Activity 1  Extensive Listening

Listen to the conversation and decide whether the following statements are true (T) or false (F).

1. This is the first-time trip. ( )
2. He should take a laptop, a cell phone and a book. ( )
3. A carry-on bag helps to save waiting time. ( )

## Activity 2　Intensive Listening

### Task 1

Listen to the conversation and answer the following questions.

1. What are they talking about?
2. What should he bring for the trip?
3. Is there any other advice?

### Task 2

Listen to the conversation again and fill in the blanks with no more than three words.

A: What should I _____ on this business trip?

B: Haven't you been on a business _____ before?

A: No. This is my _____ time.

B: You should bring your _____, cell phone, and chargers.

A: Any other _____?

B: Bring a carry-on bag only, so you don't have to wait for your luggage.

## Activity 3　Speaking

### Language Bank

When taking a business trip for the first time, you might need to ask for some advice on packing the luggage. Here are some common expressions you might use.

**Asking for packing advice:**

What should I bring for this business trip?

What are necessary to be taken for my business trip?

What can I take to the airport for this trip?

Any advice on packing for the business trip?

What else should I bring for the business trip?

**Offering advice on packing:**

You should bring…

…is/are necessary for your trip.

You'd better take…, so that you don't have to wait for your luggage.

Use the expressions above. Create your own business conversation and practice it with your partner.

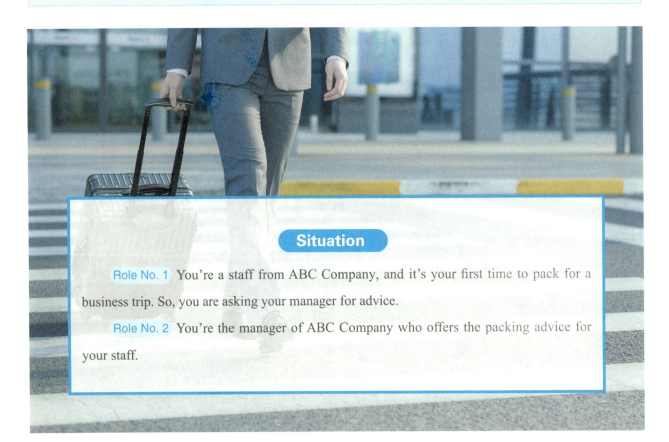

### Situation

**Role No. 1** You're a staff from ABC Company, and it's your first time to pack for a business trip. So, you are asking your manager for advice.

**Role No. 2** You're the manager of ABC Company who offers the packing advice for your staff.

Unit 4 | Traveling on Business

# Part II  Arrange the Trip

In this part, you will hear a conversation between a businessman and his secretary. This part consists of 3 activities. After each listening task, some useful language points will be discussed and you might use them in the following speaking task.

## Words and Expressions

| | | | |
|---|---|---|---|
| flight | /flaɪt/ | n. | a journey made by air, especially in a plane（尤指乘飞机的）空中航行航程 |
| requirements | /rɪˈkwaɪəmənts/ | n. | something that you need or want 需要；必需品 |
| confirmation | /ˌkɒnfəˈmeɪʃn/ | n. | a statement, letter, etc. that shows that something is true correct or definite 证实；确认书；证明书 |
| passport | /ˈpɑːspɔːt/ | n. | an official document that identifies you as a citizen of particular country, and that you may have to show when you enter or leave a country 护照 |
| leave for | | | to set out for some destination 动身去 |
| set off | | | to set in motion, cause to begin 出发，动身 |
| credit agreement | | | a contract or document containing such a money settlement 信贷协定 |
| Tokyo | /ˈtəʊkjəʊ/ | n. | the capital and largest city of Japan 东京（日本首都） |

### Activity 1 | Extensive Listening

Listen to the conversation and decide whether the following statements are true (T) or false (F).

1. They are talking about the plan for a business trip.          (     )
2. The man is going to Tokyo next month.                          (     )
3. He wants to take the flight at 10 a.m.                          (     )
4. He needs to take his sports items.                              (     )

## Activity 2　Intensive Listening

### Task 1

Listen to the conversation again and answer the following questions.

1. When will he leave for the trip?
2. Does Linda need to book a hotel room?
3. What does Linda remind him to take?

### Task 2

Listen to the conversation again and fill in the blanks with no more than three words.

A: Linda, I'm going to Tokyo on business next week.

B: When will you _____? How long will you stay?

A: I'm going to _____ on 15th and _____ on 23rd.

B: Well, I will _____ ticket and room for you. Which flight do you like?

A: The flight _____ at about 10 a.m.

B: What's your requirement about the hotel?

A: You could book the hotel which has company credit agreement with our company.

B: I got it. After I receive confirmation of the ticket and hotel, I will give you _____ about the trip agenda.

A: Please remind me to bring my passport and other important things.

B: OK.

## Activity 3　Speaking

### Language Bank

In the process of arranging a business trip, information should be offered to ensure a good trip. Here are some common expressions that might help you.

**Inquiring the trip plan and confirming it:**
When will you leave… (place)?
How long will you stay at… (place)?

Which flight/hotel do you like/prefer?

What's your favorite hotel?

After I arrange the trip, I will give you a list to let you know about it.

**Offering the trip plan:**

I am going to leave for… (places) on… (date), and come back on… (date).

The flight takes off at… (time).

I like to take the hotel with… (requirements).

Please remind me of… (documents).

Use the expressions above. Create your own business conversation and practice it with your partner.

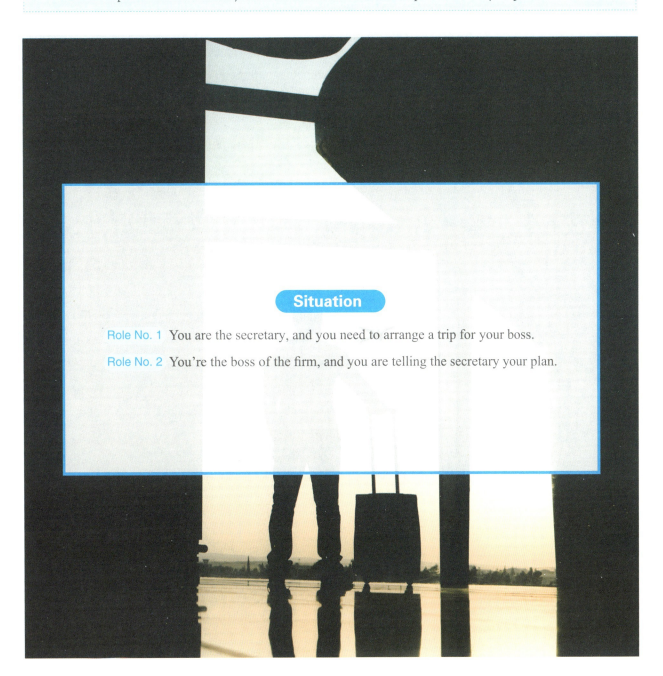

**Situation**

Role No. 1  You are the secretary, and you need to arrange a trip for your boss.

Role No. 2  You're the boss of the firm, and you are telling the secretary your plan.

# Part III  Book a Flight Online

It's a good day for Anna to take a business trip abroad (国外). First and foremost, she needs to book a flight online. With Denise's help, can she book the flight online successfully? Let's watch the video and see how to book a flight online.

| **Words and Expressions** | | | |
|---|---|---|---|
| outbound | /ˈaʊtbaʊnd/ | a. | travelling from a place rather than arriving in it 向外的；出港的；离开某地的 |
| select | /sɪˈlekt/ | v. | to choose sb./sth. from a group of people or things, usually according to a system 选择；挑选；选拔 |
| aisle | /aɪl/ | n. | a passage between rows of seats in a church, theatre, train, etc., or between rows of shelves in a supermarket（教堂、戏院、火车等位间或超级市场货架间的）走道，过道 |
| flexible | /ˈfleksəbl/ | a. | flexible object or material can be bent easily without breaking 柔韧的 |
| fixed | /fɪkst/ | a. | staying the same; not changing or able to be changed 固定的；不能变的 |
| log on | | | to perform the actions that allow you to begin using a computer system 登录，注册，进入（计算机系统） |
| business class | | | the part of a plane where passengers have a high level of comfort and service, designed for people travelling on business, and less expensive than first class（飞机上的）公务舱，商务舱 |
| economy class | | | on an aeroplane, an economy class ticket or seat is the cheapest available 经济舱 |
| Marseille | /maːˈseɪl/ | n. | a city of southeast France 马赛（法国） |
| Heathrow | /ˈhiːθrəʊ/ | n. | the airport in London 希思罗机场（英国伦敦） |

Unit 4 | Traveling on Business

## Activity 1    Extensive Watching

Watch a short video and answer the following questions.

1. What are they mainly talking about in this conversation?
2. Do they select business class or economy class?
3. Do they choose the aisle seat?

## Activity 2    Intensive Watching

### Task 1

Watch the video again and choose the correct answers.

1. When does the plane leave from Heathrow?
   A. 6 a.m.        B. 7 a.m.        C. 8 a.m.        D. 9 a.m.
2. Which is right about the booking ticket?
   A. Flexible.                     B. Fixed.
   C. Window seat.                  D. Business class.

### Task 2

Watch the video again and fill in the blanks.

A: Pull up a chair, Anna, and we'll _____. Right, let's start with the British Airlines Website. There. London to Marseille. What is the outbound _____?

B: Going out tomorrow, back tomorrow.

A: Business class or economy class? I think we'll say economy.

B: That's _____ I guess. What is this mean? Flexible or fixed?

A: A flexible ticket _____ you can change your flight but a fixed one means you can't—and that's cheaper, so we'll choose that one. I'll book you on the 8 a.m. from Heathrow and flying home at 6 p.m. I just need to _____ your full name now and select your seats. Window or aisle?

B: I'll what?

A: No, Anna. A seat by the aisle or by the _____?

B: Oh. An aisle seat please, Denise.

A: Good.

# Activity 3  Speaking

## Language Bank

If you want to book a flight online for your business trip, the following common expressions can help you.

**Beginning the booking:**

We'll log on… (website).

Let's start with… (website).

Why not have a try online?

…(website) is a large service website.

You could book the hotel/flight on… (website).

**Making choices when booking:**

What is the leaving/departure date/time?

What is the return date/time?

Do you like economy class or business class?

Would you prefer the flexible ticket or fixed one?

Do you like the aisle seat or window seat?

**Finishing the booking:**

I'll book you on… (information).

Good. Well done.

This is our flight schedule.

We have booked the flight.

### Task 1 ▶

Use the expressions you've just learned as prompts and watch the video again. Then practice the conversation with your partner.

Unit 4 | Traveling on Business

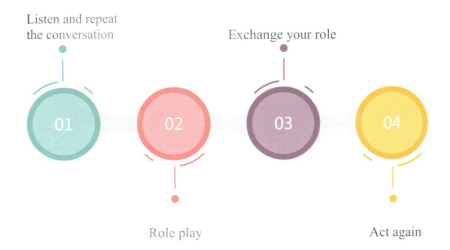

Listen and repeat the conversation — 01
Role play — 02
Exchange your role — 03
Act again — 04

## ▣ Task 2 ▶

Use the expressions above. Create your own business conversation and practice it with your group members.

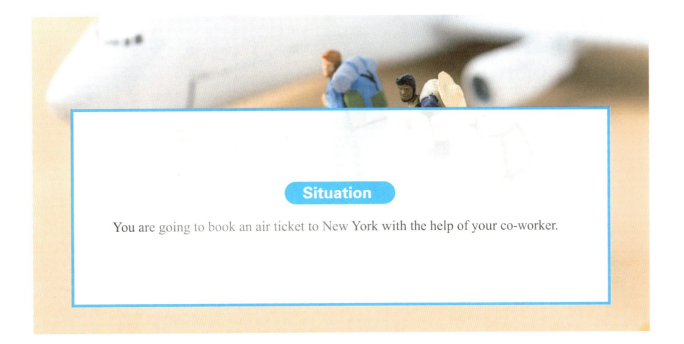

**Situation**

You are going to book an air ticket to New York with the help of your co-worker.

# Part IV  Sign a Contract

In this part, you will watch a short video on how to close a deal during the business trip. Let's watch together to see whether Tom and Anna succeed in signing a contract. This part consists of 3 tasks. After each watching and listening task, some useful language points will be discussed and you might use them in the following speaking task.

| Words and Expressions | | | |
|---|---|---|---|
| unique | /juˈniːk/ | a. | being the only one 唯一的；独一无二的 |
| curve | /kɜːv/ | n. | a line or surface that bends gradually; a smooth bend 曲线；弧线；曲面；弯曲 |
| throw in | | | to add as a supplement 免费添加 |

### Activity 1    Extensive Watching

Watch a short video and answer the following questions.

1. Where does this conversation take place?
2. What are they doing in this video?
3. Do they sign the contract finally?

### Activity 2    Intensive Watching

 Task 1

Watch the video again and choose the correct answers.

1. Which feature does NOT belong to Imperial Lemons?

   A. They are made with the unique laser curve technology.

   B. They are hard wearing.

   C. They are a joy to have on display in any shop window or restaurant.

   D. They are on the back of the box.

2. How many lemons should Mr. Brown order to sign for a good price?

   A. 10,000.　　　　B. 1,000.　　　　C. 11,000.　　　　D. 1,100.

Unit 4 | Traveling on Business

## Task 2

Watch the video again and fill in the blanks.

Anna: So, we really feel that we _____ that you'll be proud to display. And to get this fantastic price you just need to _____ of 10,000.

Tom: And we can even throw in _____ of our new Perfect Peach range.

Anna: Each lemon comes with a satisfaction guarantee. I know you won't be _____.

Brown: Hmm. It sounds good. OK, I think you _____.

Anna: OK. I _____ if you could just _____. We'll get the lemons to you as quickly as we can. Tom, do you have a pen?

Tom: Erm, no. Actually, it was in my bag yesterday but it's gone… it was a nice, a good one too.

Brown: No problem. I have a pen. _____.

Anna: Thank you. It was _____ doing business with you. We'll get those lemons to you in two weeks time.

Brown: Perfect!

## Activity 3 — Speaking

### Language Bank

There are many ways to sign a contract successfully. The following are some common expressions that might help you.

**Greeting before signing a contract:**

Good morning/afternoon/evening.

Glad/Pleased to see you. I'm… (name) in… (company).

Thank you for sparing the time to see us.

I think we should sit down and discuss business.

**Negotiating for the agreement:**

I believe... (company) has offered you a good price.

We really feel that we have a product that you'll be proud to display.

To get this fantastic price you just need to place an order of... (quantity).

Each... (product) comes with a satisfaction guarantee.

I know you won't be disappointed.

I would be grateful if you could just sign the contract.

We'll get the... (product or service) to you as quickly as we can.

**Signing the contract:**

It was a pleasure doing business with you.

We'll get those... (product) to you in... (time).

Let's sign the contract together.

Let's clinch the deal by signing it on the contract.

Congratulations on the contract!

## Task 1

Use the expressions you've just learned to complete the following conversation. Then practice it with your partner.

A: Good morning, Mr. Smith.

B: Nice to see you, Mr. David. How's your _____?

A: Perfect. Thank you for _____ the time to see me.

B: You are welcome. We appreciate that you spend time flying and visiting us.

A: I think we should _____ and discuss business.

B: Of course. Please.

A: That company has offered you many colors of carpets, but I brought the most favorite sample for you to have a close look. I believe we can _____ them.

B: That seems to meet our needs. Is it pure wool?

A: Yes. It's also a new product and is highly recommended. We really feel that we have the product that you'll be proud to _____.

B: OK. Can you supply the carpet within one week?

A: No problem. The price is the lowest. So, can we sign a contract now? I would be grateful if you could just _____.

B: That's fine. Let's make a deal.

## Task 2 ▶

Use the expressions above. Create your own business conversation and practice it with your group members.

### Situation

You're landing at 10 a.m. at Los Angeles airport. Your business partner will meet you at the airport. You are going to show him the latest product and you are confident to sign a contract.

# Project-based Task

## Objectives

1. Pack the luggage—ask for and offer the packing advice
2. Arrange the trip—inquire and give the routine
3. Book a flight online—make the decision
4. Sign a contract—negotiate for the business

## Task Background

It's a big day for Alan to plan for his first business trip to New York, US. He asked his colleague Victor for the advice on packing for the trip, and then he talked with his secretary Susan to arrange the whole plan. Getting off from the work, he surfed the internet and logged on the airline website to choose his suitable flight with his friend Haven during the dinner.

## Procedures

| | | |
|---|---|---|
| Planning |  | Discuss with group members and plan at least 3 scenarios. |
| Creating |  | Create conversations for the scenarios based on the expressions in this unit. |
| Acting |  | Choose the role you like and act out the conversations. Present the conversations in the class and make a vlog. |
| Assessing |  | Make assessment. It includes teacher's assessment (30%), self-assessment (10%), group assessment (20%), peer assessment (20%) and social assessment (20%). |

## Possible Scenarios

### Scenario 1

When Alan was informed to take a business trip to the US, he was joyful and excited. At the same time, he prepared for it carefully. The first person he asked for help is Victor, his manager. Victor has lots of travelling experience, and he is glad to share his ideas on packing the luggage with Alan.

Role No. 1  Alan: Ask the packing advice

Role No. 2  Victor: Offer his advice

Role No. 3  Colleague 1: Interrupt in by adding other information

Role No. 4  Colleague 2: Agree with Victor

### Scenario 2

After talking with Victor, Alan went to his secretary Susan to confirm the arrangements with her.

Role No. 1  Alan: Tell his arrangements

Role No. 2  Susan: Confirm the information

Role No. 3  Colleague 1: Add some information

Role No. 4  Colleague 2: Express his admiration

### Scenario 3

Alan got off the work, and he was taking supper with his friend Haven. They talked about his first business trip, and decided to choose the ticket online.

Role No. 1  Alan: Consult with Haven to book a flight online

Role No. 2  Haven: Help Alan to make the decision

Requirements:

- All group members are required to take part in the project.
- Use the expressions you have learned in this unit as many as possible.

# Self-assessment Checklist

Now, it's time for you to review your performance after learning this unit. Carry out a self-assessment by checking the following table.

| Items | | Ratings | | | |
|---|---|---|---|---|---|
| | | A | B | C | D |
| Listening Skills | I can recognize the expressions about people's identities. | | | | |
| | I can get packing information. | | | | |
| | I can get the information to arrange a trip. | | | | |
| | I can catch the information to book online. | | | | |
| | I can understand the choices of a seat. | | | | |
| | I can understand check-in information at the airport. | | | | |
| | I can understand the good wishes for a trip. | | | | |
| | I can understand expressions about signing a contract. | | | | |
| Speaking Skills | I can ask for the information about people's identities. | | | | |
| | I can ask for the advice on packing. | | | | |
| | I can inquire the arrangements about the trip. | | | | |
| | I can ask for the information to book online. | | | | |
| | I can make a decision to choose a seat. | | | | |
| | I can check in at the airport. | | | | |
| | I can express the good wishes for a trip. | | | | |
| | I can negotiate a contract. | | | | |
| Professional Skills | I can pack suitable luggage to begin business travel. | | | | |
| | I can plan an itinerary to arrange business travel. | | | | |
| | I can book online ticket to ensure business travel. | | | | |
| | I can sign a contract to conclude business travel. | | | | |

A: Basically agree

B: Agree

C: Strongly agree

D: Disagree

# Overview

Hotel communication skills are an inseparable (不可分离的) element in daily life, hospitality industry as well as business world. Whether going on a business trip or receiving foreign clients, hotel is always our first choice for accommodation. Sometimes we even hold company annual parties at a hotel, too. During the stay, you may run into hotel problems from checking in to checking out, from requiring service to making complaints. Learning how to express yourself and handle different situations at a hotel is an important step in a business trip. Therefore, in this unit, we will learn **how to check in, enquire hotel service, complain about a hotel, and check out.** Now let us start our business journey!

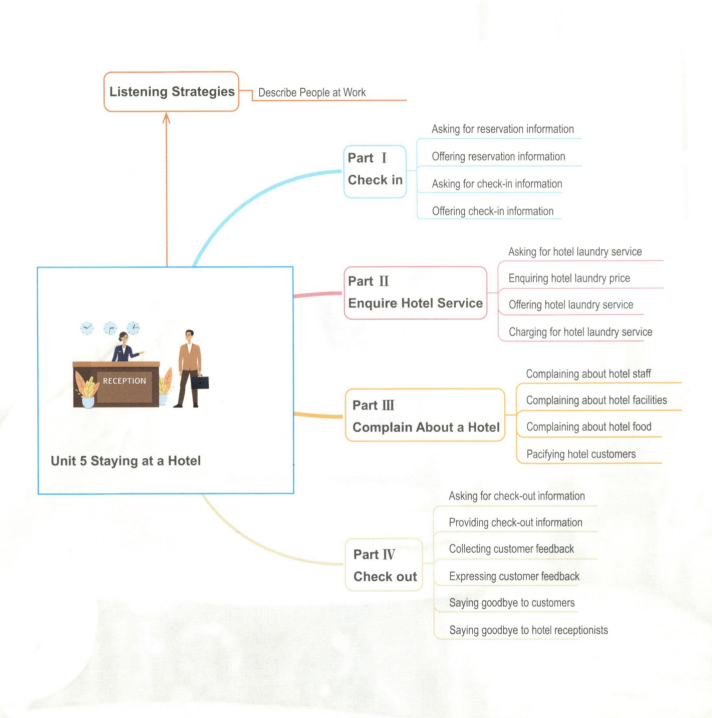

# Understanding Describing People

How would you introduce a person? We usually describe someone by his name, appearance and personality. However, in business situation, apart from following the introduction sequence of business etiquette (礼节), we should pay attention to the way of describing a person's name, job title, organization and personality. Here is the sequence and tips for describing people.

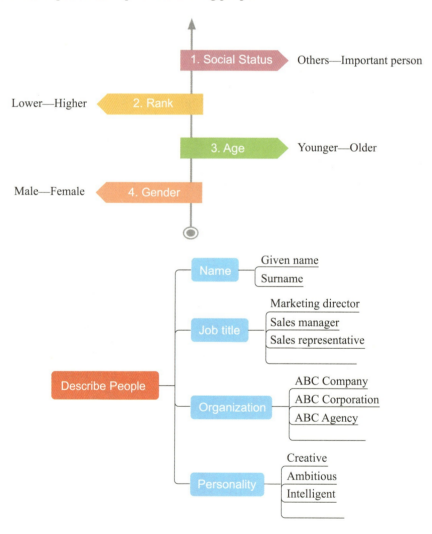

Here are some typical expressions to describe people.

## Describe People at Work

1. Let me introduce ×××. He is the chief manager from ABC Company.
2. He is our new colleague, ×××. He just started as a sales assistant in the marketing department.
3. This is ×××. She is in charge of exports.
4. His name is ×××, and he is a director at ABC Electronic Factory.
5. He currently works as a marketing manager in the trade department at ABC Import Corporation.
6. I've been working in marketing for about 20 years.
7. ××× is good at dealing with this situation. She is highly competent.
8. My boss is always polite and considerate (体谅的) towards us.
9. ××× is our senior employee. He is very reliable. You can trust him.
10. I enjoy working with ××× because she is so easy-going.

### Task

Listen to the conversation and fill in the blanks. You can try to review the expressions to help you understand describing people.

#### Conversation 1

Manager: Good morning, everyone. _____ introduce Mary, our new _____. She used to work at a _____.

Mary: Good morning, my name is Mary. I've been _____ this field for 10 years. I hope we can _____ each other.

#### Conversation 2

Lily: Lucy, what do you think of our new manager, Tom? He is _____, isn't he?

Lucy: Yes, he works as a _____ for 10 years. He is _____ and _____. He always gives us amazing plans. We can _____ him.

#### Conversation 3

Mike: Hi, Judy. We haven't met each other since the _____ last year.

Judy: Hello, Mike. Nice to see you again. Is he a _____ in your company? I've never seen him before.

Mike: Yes, this is _____, Tom. He is our new staff and _____ a marketing assistant in the _____. He is _____ and _____. Tom, this is Judy. She is a marketing manager from ABC Company's _____. We are _____ and _____ for over 10 years.

Tom: Nice to meet you, Mrs. Judy.

Mike: Nice to meet you, too.

# Lead-in

## Cultural Background

Are you always satisfied with the hotel that you lived in when you're on a business trip? Have you ever met some troubles while staying at a hotel? What factors (因素) will influence your choice of a hotel? We believe that every businessman needs a comfortable, convenient and qualified accommodation. For the business travelers, a better hotel experience will bring to a higher work efficiency. Let's look at the top 10 things that business travelers want from hotels.

**Proximity (靠近).** Hotel locations stand the top priority. A good location means business travelers could save more time on the road, thus gainning more time to finish their task.

**A Personalized Experience.** An intelligent hotel app can not only understand business travelers' needs and preferences, but also offer automated booking, check-in and check-out service.

**Free (and Fast) Wi-Fi.** Free Wi-Fi is a must. The quicker, the better. It will be great if the corporate travel agents can help save the upcharge (附加费用) fee of a faster connection service.

**Plenty of Power Outlets (插座).** Business travelers need more power outlets for their mobile phones, tablets, laptops and even irons.

**Accessible Meeting Rooms.** A well-equipped conference room is essential to share ideas, enhance cooperation and secure new clients.

**Fast Service.** Compared to normal customers, business travelers are eager for faster and more effective service, such as room service, dry-cleaning and shoeshine (擦鞋) service.

**Healthy Hotel Dinning Options.** A healthy diet helps to balance out the food that business travelers eat at the airport or with their business clients.

**Easy Fitness Opportunities.** What business travelers want is a large, well-marked and well-maintained fitness center, so that they can get a work-out.

**A Setting that Promotes Productivity and Rest.** Convenient facilities like business center can improve work productivity. Quiet and large room can ensure the quality of sleep.

**Somewhere to Relax and Unwind (放松).** Public activity space is a great place for business travelers to go for a walk and relax themselves.

### Task 1

Read the above passage and answer the following questions.

1. For business travelers, what kind of fast service is needed?
2. Why should the hotel provide a healthy dinning option for business travelers?

### Task 2

Think about the following questions and discuss in small groups.

1. What will influence your choice of a hotel?
2. What kind of hotel service is a must for business travelers?

# Warm-up

## Word Search

When you saw the phrase "staying at a hotel", what's the first word that occurs to you? Here we have some common words which are relevant to our topic in the crossword. This crossword consists of a few words Across (C) and a few words Down (D). Review the clues for each word and fill in the corresponding boxes with the letters that spell out the word! Can you write down all the words? Please share your answer with your classmates when you've finished it.

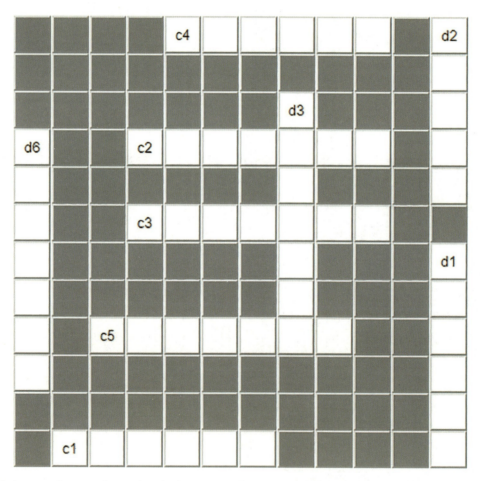

c1. A room where people can sit and relax
c2. Convenient facilities
c3. An acknowledgment that payment has been made
c4. An amount of money that you have to pay for a service
c5. A workplace where clothes are washed and ironed

d1. Postpone indefinitely or annul something that was scheduled
d2. The place you live during your business trip
d3. A small refrigerator
d6. A kind of public transport

# Business Communication

## Part I Check in

In this part, you will hear a hotel check-in conversation between two native speakers. They ask and offer basic check-in information. This part consists of 3 activities. After each listening task, some useful language points will be discussed, and you might use them in the following speaking task.

### Words and Expressions

| | | | |
|---|---|---|---|
| reservation | /ˌrezəˈveɪʃn/ | n. | If you make a reservation, you arrange for something such as a table in a restaurant or a room in a hotel to be kept for you. 预订 |
| sign | /saɪn/ | v. | When you sign a document, you write your name on it, usually at the end or in a special space. 签名 |
| check in | | | to register at a hotel 登记；办理入住手续 |

### Activity 1   Extensive Listening

Listen to the conversation and decide whether the following statements are true (T) or false (F).

1. Jackson had made a reservation.　　　　　　　　　　　　　　　（　）
2. Jackson wants a double room.　　　　　　　　　　　　　　　　（　）
3. Jackson wants a smoking room.　　　　　　　　　　　　　　　　（　）

## Activity 2  Intensive Listening

### Task 1

Listen to the conversation and answer the following questions.

1. How would Jackson like to pay?
2. What is the price for a night?
3. What is his room number?

### Task 2

Listen to the conversation again and fill in the blanks with no more than three words.

Receptionist: Good morning, sir. Welcome to the Belleclaire Hotel. How may I help you?

Frank: Good morning. I'd like to check in, please. I have a _____ under the name Jackson.

Receptionist: Certainly, sir. May I have your _____, please?

Frank: Here you are.

Receptionist: Thank you.

Receptionist: Ah, here we are, Mr. Frank Jackson. A _____ room for three nights, is that correct?

Frank: Yes, I'll be checking out on the 9th.

Receptionist: Would you like a smoking or _____ room?

Frank: Smoking, please.

Receptionist: Will you be paying _____ or by card?

Frank: I'll pay by visa if that's OK.

Receptionist: Yes, certainly Mr. Jackson. That's £84 per night, _____ total. You can pay on check out if you'd like.

Frank: Sure.

Receptionist: If you could just write your name and email, and then sign here… and here.

Receptionist: Thank you. Here's your passport, and this is your _____. Room 237. Breakfast is included and is served in the _____ between 7 and 10 a.m.

Frank: Thank you.

Unit 5 | Staying at a Hotel

### Activity 3 | Speaking

## Language Bank

Before checking in a hotel, most people will make a reservation online or by phone call first, just to make sure the room is available. After that, they will go to the hotel to check-in and pay for the rate. How will they communicate with the hotel receptionist? Here are some common expressions that might help you.

**Asking for reservation information:**

What kind of room are you looking for?
When would you like to check in?
For how many people?

**Offering reservation information:**

I'd like to make a reservation for… (date) for one night, please.
I'd like a single/double/twin/triple/suite room with a… view for… nights.

**Asking for check-in information:**

Good morning. Welcome to ABC Hotel. How may I help you?
May I have your passport/identification, please?
A… room for… nights, is that correct?
Will you be paying by… or by…?
Do I need to pay a deposit?
Where is my room?

**Offering check-in information:**

I'd like to check in. I have a reservation under the name of…
I will pay by cash/visa/credit card if that's OK.
Yes, a deposit of… is required.
This is your keycard. Room 601, on 6th floor.

Use the expressions above. Create your own business conversation and practice it with your partner.

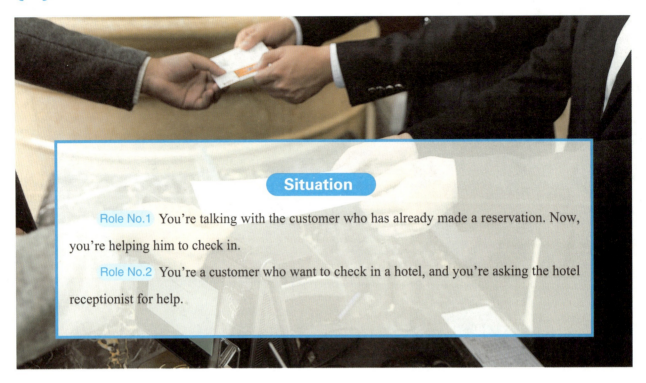

### Situation

**Role No.1** You're talking with the customer who has already made a reservation. Now, you're helping him to check in.

**Role No.2** You're a customer who want to check in a hotel, and you're asking the hotel receptionist for help.

# Part II  Enquire Hotel Service

In this part, you will hear a conversation between a customer and hotel clerks. They're talking about hotel service. This part consists of 3 activities. After each listening task, some useful language points will be discussed and you might use them in the following speaking task.

### Words and Expressions

| | | | |
|---|---|---|---|
| laundry | /ˈlɔːndrɪ/ | n. | It is used to refer to clothes, sheets, and towels that are about to be washed, are being washed, or have just been washed.（待洗、正在洗或刚洗过的）衣物 |
| press | /pres/ | v. | If you press clothes, you iron them in order to get rid of the creases. 熨 |
| room service | | | It is a service in a hotel by which meals or drinks are provided for guests in their rooms.（宾馆的）客房服务 |
| fill out | | | If you fill out a form or other document requesting information, you write information in the spaces on it. 填写 |

## Activity 1 | Extensive Listening

Listen to the conversation and decide whether the following statements are true (T) or false (F).

1. The customer wants a laundry service. ( )
2. The customer needs her suit pressed. ( )
3. The customer can get her shirts back tomorrow evening. ( )

## Activity 2 | Intensive Listening

### Task 1 ▶

Listen to the conversation again and answer the following questions.

1. Why does the customer call?
2. How long will it take to press the suit?
3. When can the customer get her clothes back?

### Task 2 ▶

Listen to the conversation again and fill in the blanks with no more than three words.

Clerk: _____ service. What can I do for you?

Val: I have some _____ that need laundering and I'd like my suit pressed.

Clerk: There's a _____ as well as a bag in your room. Please _____ and put it together with the clothes into the bag, and the _____ will come and pick it up.

Val: How long will it take to get my clothes back?

Clerk: To _____ the suit only takes three hours. The laundry will be returned to you tomorrow around _____ time. Is that all right?

Val: That's all right. Please send someone to pick it up.

Clerk: Right away, sir.

Clerk: Laundry service. May I come in?

Val: Please. These are my shirts that need laundering. One of them _____, be sure to wash it carefully.

Clerk: Don't worry. We promise a new shirt will be back to you.

## Activity 3　Speaking

## Language Bank

When staying at a hotel, you may ask hotel service like taxi-hailing, morning call, food ordering, laundry, entertainment and so on. Here are some common expressions that might help you when you want to enquire hotel laundry service.

**Asking for hotel laundry service:**

How long will it take to get my clothes back?
When can I have my laundry back?
Where can I find the laundry bag?
I have some… that need laundering and I'd like my… pressed. Could you send someone up for my laundry, please?
Do you have express laundry service? I need my dress this evening.

**Enquiring hotel laundry price:**

How much do you charge for express laundry service?
How about the rate?
Can you explain the detailed laundry price?

**Offering hotel laundry service:**

Room service. What can I do for you?
Laundry service. May I come in?
Do you have any special request?
When do you want them back, sir?
If you have any dirty clothes, please just leave it in the laundry bag behind the bathroom door.
It takes one day to have the laundry done.
Please tell us or notify in the list whether you need your clothes ironed, washed, dry-cleaned or mended, and also what time you want to get them back.

**Charging for hotel laundry service:**

We can deliver it within 4 hours at a 60% extra charge.
We charge 50% more for express laundry service.

Use the expressions above. Create your own business conversation and practice it with your partner.

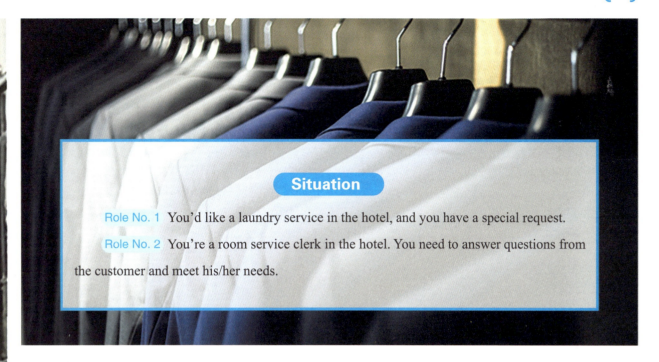

**Situation**

Role No. 1  You'd like a laundry service in the hotel, and you have a special request.

Role No. 2  You're a room service clerk in the hotel. You need to answer questions from the customer and meet his/her needs.

# Part III  Complain About a Hotel

A customer is annoyed at the hotel staff. Finally, she decides to complain about the terrible service to the hotel manager. Why did the madam get angry and what does the manger do to pacify (安抚) her?

## Words and Expressions

| | | | |
|---|---|---|---|
| staff | /stɑːf/ | n. | The personnel of an organization are the people who work for it. 全体职员 |
| disappointed | /ˌdɪsəˈpɔɪntɪd/ | a. | If you are disappointed, you are sad because something has not happened or because something is not as good as you had hoped. 失望的 |
| ignore | /ɪgˈnɔː(r)/ | v. | If you ignore someone or something, you pay no attention to them. 不理睬 |
| hire | /ˈhaɪə(r)/ | v. | If you hire someone, you employ them or pay them to do a particular job for you. 雇用 |
| instruct | /ɪnˈstrʌkt/ | v. | If you instruct someone to do something, you formally tell them to do it. 指示；吩咐 |
| concierge | /ˈkɒnsɪeəʒ/ | n. | It refers to an employee of a hotel who assists guests. 旅馆服务员 |
| reception | /rɪˈsepʃn/ | n. | It is the desk or office that books rooms for people and answers their questions.（酒店）接待处；服务台 |

| Activity 1 | Extensive Watching |

Watch a short video and answer the following questions.

1. When does the conversation take place?
2. What are they mainly talking about?
3. What does the hotel manager do to pacify the customer?

| Activity 2 | Intensive Watching |

### Task 1

Watch the video again and choose the correct answers.

1. Why did the customer feel angry?
   A. The hotel staff didn't hear her voice.
   B. The hotel staff guided her a wrong place.
   C. The hotel staff couldn't understand her.
   D. The hotel staff's voice was too low to be heard.

2. Why did the hotel staff make mistakes?
   A. He just came to work here.
   B. He was sick.
   C. He was in bad temper.
   D. He is a temporary staff.

### Task 2

Watch the video again and fill in the blanks.

A: Excuse me, are you the manager of this hotel?

B: Good evening, madam. I am Narita, the manager. How may I help you?

A: I was _____ with your staff. At first, I asked for his help, but he _____ me. And then I asked toward the restaurant _____, but he directed me in wrong place. How could you _____ staff like him?

B: I am sorry, madam. He is Adam. He is our new staff. He came here two days ago. One of our staff was sick, so I don't have a _____ but to let him in the floor. But I _____ him to _____ only. Any of the guests asked him immediately direct them to the _____.

A: You should not let him alone. Train him before letting him go to work.

B: Once again, madam. I do apologize in his _____, it was our fault. I will not let these things happen again.

A: All right.

B: Thank you for your understanding. You can call me direct in the _____ if you need any help.

A: No, I'm fine. Thank you.

## Activity 3　Speaking

## Language Bank

> If you want to make some complaints about a hotel, whether its staff, facilities or food, you can use some common expressions as follows.

**Complaining about hotel staff:**

I was disappointed with your staff.
I asked for his help, but he ignored me.
I think he made a mistake with my room reservation.
How could you hire staff like him?

**Complaining about hotel facilities:**

We requested a non-smoking room, but the room smells of smoke.
There are no towels/toiletry items/toilet paper in the bathroom.
The air conditioner is not working properly.

**Complaining about hotel food:**

There's a worm in my dish.
This steak is raw. I asked for well-done! And it's rather cold.
The boiled potatoes are almost raw. They are so hard. It's like they haven't cooked the potatoes at all.

**Pacifying hotel customers:**

How may I help you?
I'm really sorry about this.
I do apologize in…
It was our fault. I will not let these things happen again.
I'm sorry for the inconvenience, sir.
Thank you for your understanding.

### Task 1

Role play. Use the expressions you've just learned as prompts and watch the video again. Then practice the conversation with your partner.

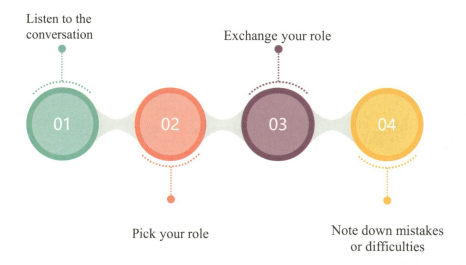

01 Listen to the conversation
02 Pick your role
03 Exchange your role
04 Note down mistakes or difficulties

### Task 2

Use the expressions above. Create your own business conversation and practice it with your group members.

**Situation**

You're complaining about the hotel staff as well as the room facilities to the hotel manager. And the manager tries her best to pacify you.

# Part IV  Check out

In this part, you will watch a short video about conversations between a hotel receptionist and a customer. In the video, they are talking about hotel check-out matters. This part consists of 3 tasks. After each watching and listening task, some useful language points will be discussed, and you might use them in the following speaking task.

### Words and Expressions

| | | | |
|---|---|---|---|
| shuttle | /ˈʃʌtl/ | n. | It is a plane, bus, or train which makes frequent trips between two places. 穿梭班机；穿梭班车；穿梭火车 |
| approximately | /əˈprɒksɪmətlɪ/ | ad. | (of quantities) imprecise but fairly close to correct 大约 |
| lounge | /laʊndʒ/ | n. | In a hotel, club, or other public place, a lounge is a room where people can sit and relax. 休息厅 |
| minibar | /ˈmɪnɪbɑː(r)/ | n. | In a hotel room, a minibar is a small refrigerator containing alcoholic drinks. 迷你吧（指宾馆里放有酒类饮料的小冰箱） |
| receipt | /rɪˈsiːt/ | n. | It is a piece of paper that you get from someone as proof that they have received money or goods from you. 收据 |
| charge | /tʃɑːdʒ/ | n. | It is an amount of money that you have to pay for a service. 费用 |
| guest book | | | It is a book in which guests write their names and addresses when they have been staying in someone's house or in a hotel. 宾客登记簿 |

## Activity 1  Extensive Watching

Watch a short video and answer the following questions.

1. How will the customer go to the airport?
2. Will the customer pay extra bill?
3. Who can help the customer with his luggage?

## Activity 2  Intensive Watching

### Task 1

Watch the video again and choose the correct answers.

1. How long will it take from the hotel to the airport?

   A. About 20 minutes.    B. About 25 minutes.    C. About 28 minutes.    D. About 23 minutes.

2. What kind of bill should the customer pay?

   A. Minibar.    B. Maintenance (维修).    C. Souvenir (纪念品).    D. Envelope.

### Task 2

Watch the video again and fill in the blanks.

A: Did you enjoy your stay with us?

B: Yes, very much so. However, I now need to get to the airport. I have a _____ that leaves in about three hours. So, what is the quickest way to get there?

A: We do have a free airport _____ service.

B: That sounds great. But will it get me to the airport on time?

A: Yes, it should. The next shuttle leaves in 15 minutes and it takes _____ 25 minutes to get to the airport.

B: Fantastic. I'll just wait in the _____ area. Will you please let me know when it will be leaving?

A: Of course, sir. Oh, before you go, would you be able to settle the _____?

B: Oh yes, certainly. How much will that be?

A: Let's see. The bill comes to 40 dollars. How would you like to pay for that?

B: I'll pay with my _____, thanks. But I'll need a _____. So, I can _____ it to my company.

A: Absolutely, here we are, sir. If you like, you can leave your bags with the _____, and he can load them onto the shuttle for you when it arrives.

B: That would be great. Thank you.

A: Would you like to sign the hotel _____ too while you wait?

B: Sure, I had a really good stay here and I'll tell other people to come here.

A: That's good to hear. Thank you again for staying at the Grand Sultan Hotel.

# Language Bank

In the hotel, when you want to check out, how can you communicate with the hotel receptionist? You can use some common expressions as follows.

### Asking for check-out information:

Are you ready to check out? What room were you in?

Would you settle the minibar/extra bill?

Do you need a taxi or any help with your bags?

I'll just need your room keys, please.

### Providing check-out information:

Sorry, I know we're a few minutes late for the check out. I'm afraid we overslept/slept in.

I'd like to check out now/we're checking out of room 612. Here is the key to my room.

There is an extra room charge on your bill. So, the total comes to $100, including tax.

I will pay with my visa/credit card.

I need a receipt. So, I can charge it to my company.

We do offer/have a free airport shuttle service.

You can leave your bags with a porter.

### Collecting customer feedback:

Did you enjoy your stay with us?

Was everything satisfactory?

Would you like to sign the hotel guest book?

### Expressing customer feedback:

I enjoy my stay for the most part. The room was great. The beds were really comfortable.

I'd be willing to try this hotel again, if you can promise me no more cockroaches.

### Saying goodbye to customers:

Thank you again for staying at… hotel. I hope you will be back to visit us again soon. Have a safe trip home.

### Saying goodbye to hotel receptionists:

I had a really good/pleasant stay here and I'll tell other people to come here.

If I am in town again for business, I'll be sure to come back.

## Activity 3　Speaking

### Task 1

Use the expressions you've just learned to complete the following conversation. Then practice it with your partner.

A: Sorry, I know we're a few minutes late for the _____. I'm afraid we _____.

B: That's no problem, madam. Which room were you in? I'll just need your room _____, please.

A: Room 612. Sure, here you are.

B: There is an extra room _____ on your _____. So, the total comes to $100, including _____.

A: I will pay with credit card and I need a _____.

B: Sure, do you need a taxi or any help with your _____?

A: No. Thank you.

B: Was everything _____?

A: I enjoy my stay for the most part. The beds were really _____.

B: Thank you again for staying at ABC Hotel.

A: Thank you.

### Task 2

Use the expressions above. Create your own business conversation and practice it with your group members.

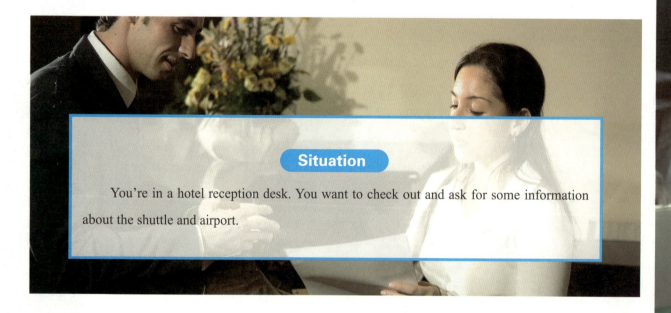

**Situation**

You're in a hotel reception desk. You want to check out and ask for some information about the shuttle and airport.

# Project-based Task

## Objectives

1. Make a hotel reservation, claim your special request and check in

2. Enquire about detailed hotel service and facilities

3. Complain about hotel service and facilities, express dissatisfaction or give advice

4. Discuss the rate, ask for traffic information and check out

## Task Background

Sophia travelled to another country for business. She called a hotel in advance to reserve a room, but at hotel reception desk, she found there's something wrong with her reservation. During her stay, she also met a series of troubles. On the check-out day, she argued with a hotel waiter and was thus late for the check-out time. So, she made a complaint to the hotel manager after checkout.

## Procedures

Planning | Discuss with group members and plan at least 3 scenarios.

Creating | Create conversations for the scenarios based on the expressions in this unit.

Acting | Choose the role you like and act out the conversations. Present the conversations in the class and make a vlog.

Assessing | Make assessment. It includes teacher's assessment (30%), self-assessment (10%), group assessment (20%), peer assessment (20%) and social assessment (20%).

## Possible Scenarios

### Scenario 1

Sophia called a hotel to book a non-smoking single room with a sea view for three nights. But when she is checking in, she finds the hotel receptionist confusing her name with another guest…

**Role No. 1** Sophia: Call to make a reservation; claim your requirements and check in.

**Role No. 2** Hotel receptionist A: Answer Sophia's reservation call; ask for her personal information and reserve the room she wants.

**Role No. 3** Hotel receptionist B: Receive Sophia but confuse her personal reservation information with another Sophia.

### Scenario 2

Sophia comes to the hotel reception desk again to enquire internet service, laundry service and food service. She also wants to know more about the hotel gym.

**Role No. 1** Sophia: Enquire hotel service and facilities.

**Role No. 2** Hotel receptionist: Offer service that Sophia wants, and introduce a well-equipped hotel gym to her.

### Scenario 3

Sophia was dissatisfied with the hotel breakfast and its rate. Besides, she was annoyed at the hotel dining hall waiter, who was unprofessional and impatient. That's why she was late for the check-out time. But the hotel receptionist asked for an upcharge. So, she found the hotel manager to complain.

**Role No. 1** Sophia: Feel dissatisfied with the breakfast; provide personal checkout information; argue the late-checkout upcharge; complain to the hotel manager.

**Role No. 2** Hotel waiter: Provide food service to Sophia.

**Role No. 3** Hotel receptionist: Ask for check out information; explain extra rate.

**Role No. 4** Hotel manager: Apologize and provide solutions; tell Sophia how to take a shuttle.

Requirements:

- All group members are required to take part in the project.
- Use the expressions you have learned in this unit as many as possible.

# Self-assessment Checklist

Now, it's time for you to review your performance after learning this unit. Carry out a self-assessment by checking the following table.

| Items | | Ratings | | | |
|---|---|---|---|---|---|
| | | A | B | C | D |
| Listening Skills | I can recognize the expressions about describing people. | | | | |
| | I can understand personal information when I check in and check out a hotel. | | | | |
| | I can understand hotel rate and upcharge issues. | | | | |
| | I can understand hotel service and options for facilities. | | | | |
| | I can understand explanation for hotel complaints. | | | | |
| | I can understand apologies for hotel complaints. | | | | |
| | I can understand hotel customer feedback. | | | | |
| | I can understand check-out procedures. | | | | |
| Speaking Skills | I can describe a person. | | | | |
| | I can ask for reservation information. | | | | |
| | I can ask for check-in information. | | | | |
| | I can enquire hotel laundry price. | | | | |
| | I can ask for hotel food service. | | | | |
| | I can complain about hotel staff, facilities and food. | | | | |
| | I can provide check-out information. | | | | |
| | I can say goodbye to hotel receptionists. | | | | |
| Professional Skills | I can reserve a hotel room, make a special request and check in. | | | | |
| | I can enquire hotel service and facilities. | | | | |
| | I can complain about hotel staff, facilities, service and food. | | | | |
| | I can check out and pay my bill. | | | | |

A: Basically agree

B: Agree

C: Strongly agree

D: Disagree

Unit **6**

**Receiving Clients**

## Overview

Receiving clients is unavoidable (不可避免的) in business field. It can help us to give a sound impression on our clients. Every step we take may influence their choices as well as the company's image. That's why it's necessary for us to be considerate and well-prepared. For example, we can set up detailed reception itineraries as well as simulate (模拟) airport pickup and see off scenes to make clients feel at home. Therefore, in this unit, we will learn **how to arrange receptions, pick up clients at the airport (on behalf of the superior), pick up clients at the airport (personally), and receive clients at the office**. Now let us start our business journey!

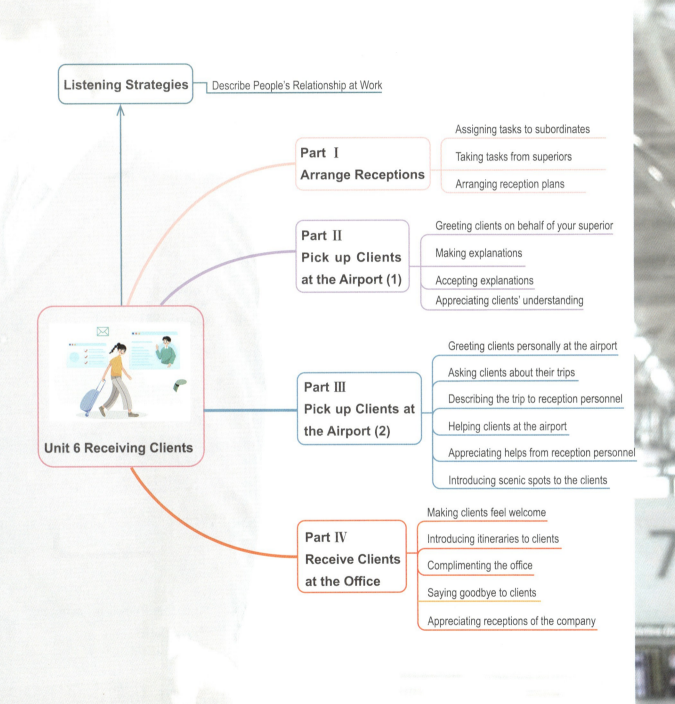

# Understanding People's Relationship

When introducing someone to others, apart from introducing his name, job title, organization and personality, we also need to describe our relationship to others. In this part, we will learn how to understand people's relationship at work. Here are two steps.

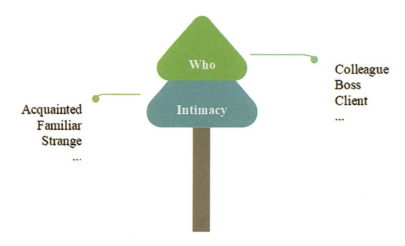

Here are some typical expressions to describe people's relationship.

## Describe People's Relationship at Work

1. This is my new team member, Mike.
2. Mr. Edward, this is Ken, my new associate.
3. Alice, I'd like you to meet Mike. He is the marketing manager of ABC Firm. Mike, this is my assistant, Alice.
4. This is Emma Lin. She is from our office in Shanghai. She is a designer.
5. Emma, allow me to introduce Ken. He works as a programmer in our headquarters (总部).
6. Good morning, everyone. Today, I will introduce a new colleague to you all.
7. If you have any problems with the report, feel free to ask Lily, my assistant.
8. May I introduce my colleague, Lily White?

9. Welcome to London, Mike. You haven't met my secretary, Anna.

10. He is my roommate, a human resource officer in our factory.

## Task

Listen to the conversation and fill in the blanks. You can try to review the expressions to help you understand the relationship between these speakers.

### Conversation 1

Mr. Brown: Good morning, Lisa.

Lisa: Good morning, Mr. Brown.

Mr. Brown: I'd like you to _____ our _____, Lily.

Lisa: Nice to meet you, Lily.

Lily: Me, too, Lisa.

Mr. Brown: Lily is our _____. So, I hope you can show her _____.

### Conversation 2

Tom: Good afternoon, I don't think we've met before. May I introduce myself? I'm Tom Smith from Eastlake _____.

Lucy: Nice to meet you, Tom. My name is Lucy Wang. Allow me to introduce my _____ from _____, Marry White.

Tom: Well, actually we've already known each other for 10 years. She is my _____. Hello, Marry. How are you?

Marry: Hello, Tom. Glad to meet you here.

### Conversation 3

Linda: I would like to introduce you to Mr. John, our _____. Mr. John, this is Mr. Robert, my colleague. He is a _____ from Green _____.

Robert: Nice to meet you, Mr. John.

John: Nice to meet you too, Mr. Robert. Welcome to our city. How was your _____?

Robert: Thank you. It's _____.

John: Let me help you with your _____.

Robert: Thank you, John.

Linda: Our car is in the _____. We've _____ ABC Hotel for you, which is behind our _____. Let's get you to the hotel.

# Lead-in

## Cultural Background

Business small talk is a light and informal conversation conducted in the business setting. It plays a vital role in situations where silence would be embarrassed and uncomfortable, but where profound and private conversations would be inappropriate (不合适的). So, when we are picking up clients at the airport or even receiving clients at our office, how could we break the ice with small talk?

Here are things that we could talk about:

**Weather.** This is a common topic which is not offensive (冒犯的) and everyone can involve into the discussion.

**Work.** Asking questions like how your clients start their line of work to show your interest to them.

**Travel.** Travel experience or travel plans are common topics in business small talk.

**Celebrities' Trivia.** Talking about latest must-see dramas, reality shows and films is also a good beginning.

**Nearby Restaurants.** When a foreign client comes to visit you, apart from business affairs, what interests him most is the cuisine. So, why not recommend him the nearby local restaurants, bars or street food?

**Local News.** Talking about local news shows that you are interested in local affairs and well-informed.

**Something that Just Happened.** You can start a conversation with what you both have heard or experienced. But remember, talk less, listen more.

### Task 1 ▶

Read the above passage and answer the following questions.

1. What is small talk?
2. List three things that we could say in small talk.

### Task 2 ▶

Think about the following questions and discuss in small groups.

1. Why do we need small talk?
2. What kind of topics should be avoided in small talk?

## Warm-up

### Word Search

When you saw the phrase "receiving client", what's the first word that occurs to you? Maybe, "airport" or "office", etc. Let's look at the word search below. Can you find out all the common words about receiving client? Feel free to use some colorful mark pens to draw circles. You can circle the words horizontally, vertically or diagonally across the grid. After drawing, please share your word search with your classmates.

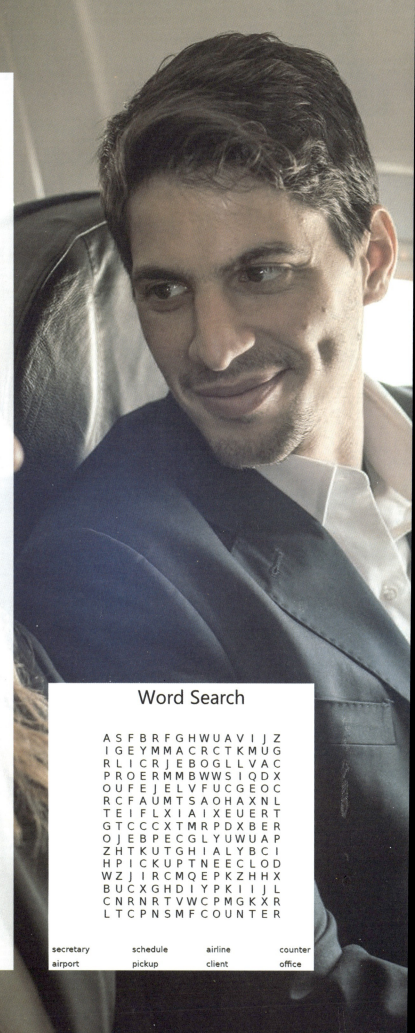

### Word Search

```
A S F B R F G H W U A V I J Z
I G E Y M M A C R C T K M U G
R L I C R J E B O G L L V A C
P R O E R M M B W W S I Q D X
O U F E J E L V F U C G E O C
R C F A U M T S A O H A X N L
T E I F L X I A I X E U E R T
G T C C C X T M R P D X B E R
O J E B P E C G L Y U W U A P
Z H T K U T G H I A L Y B C I
H P I C K U P T N E E C L O D
W Z J I R C M Q E P K Z H H X
B U C X G H D I Y P K I I J L
C N R N R T V W C P M G K X R
L T C P N S M F C O U N T E R
```

| secretary | schedule | airline | counter |
| airport | pickup | client | office |

# Business Communication

## Part I Arrange Receptions

In this part, you will hear a business conversation between two native speakers. They are talking in the company. This part consists of 3 activities. After each listening task, some useful language points will be discussed and you might use them in the following speaking task.

### Words and Expressions

| | | | |
|---|---|---|---|
| schedule | /ˈʃedjuːl/ | n. | It is a plan which gives a list of events or tasks and the times at which each one should happen or be done. 日程安排 |
| airline | /ˈeəlaɪn/ | n. | It is a company that provides regular services carrying people or goods in aeroplanes. 航空公司 |
| arrival time | | | the time at which a public conveyance is scheduled to arrive at a given destination 到达时间 |

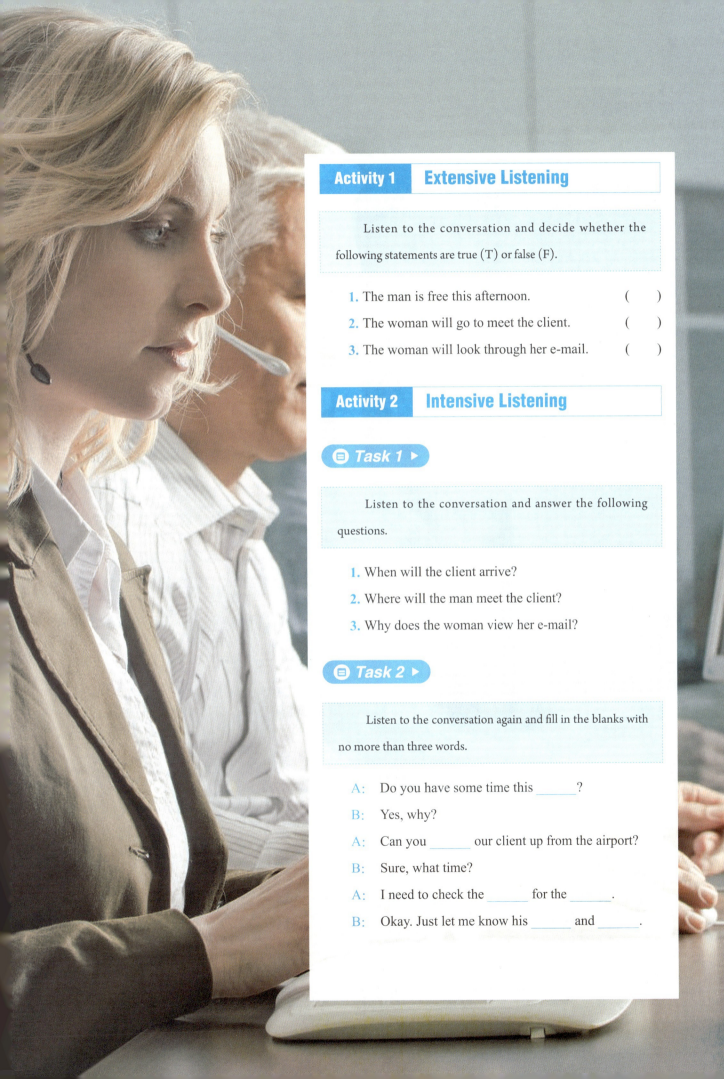

**Activity 1  Extensive Listening**

Listen to the conversation and decide whether the following statements are true (T) or false (F).

1. The man is free this afternoon.　　　　　　(   )
2. The woman will go to meet the client.　　　(   )
3. The woman will look through her e-mail.　 (   )

**Activity 2  Intensive Listening**

● Task 1 ▶

Listen to the conversation and answer the following questions.

1. When will the client arrive?
2. Where will the man meet the client?
3. Why does the woman view her e-mail?

● Task 2 ▶

Listen to the conversation again and fill in the blanks with no more than three words.

A: Do you have some time this _____?
B: Yes, why?
A: Can you _____ our client up from the airport?
B: Sure, what time?
A: I need to check the _____ for the _____.
B: Okay. Just let me know his _____ and _____.

| Activity 3 | Speaking |

## Language Bank

> When assigning your subordinate (下属) a task, do give him clear information about the exact work, especially the time and place. Here are some common expressions that might help you.

**Assigning tasks to subordinates:**

Do you have time this afternoon? Can you pick our clients up from the airport?

I will give you a rush job, and you have to finish it before you leave.

You need to meet the new client at the airport. He will arrive at 6 p.m.

Please book a hotel suite room for our business associate.

Are you clear about everything?

**Taking tasks from superiors (上级):**

What do you want to see me about?

Sure, just let me know his airline and arrival time.

I will finish the task as soon as possible.

OK. I will book him a hotel suite room right now.

All right. I will submit a detailed reception itinerary to you.

**Arranging reception plans:**

Check your e-mail to confirm the airline and flight schedule.

Make sure you arrive at the airport in advance.

Borrow the company car to pick up client.

Take the client to dinner and then drive him to the hotel.

> Use the expressions above. Create your own business conversation and practice it with your partner.

### Situation

**Role No. 1** You're assigned to pick up a client tomorrow morning, and now you're discussing a detailed pick-up plan with your superior.

**Role No. 2** You're a manager and you're assigning your assistant to pick up a client at the airport.

# Part II  Pick up Clients at the Airport (1)

In this part, you will hear a business conversation between two native speakers. They're greeting at the airport. This part consists of 3 activities. After each listening task, some useful language points will be discussed and you might use them in the following speaking task.

## Words and Expressions

| secretary | /ˈsekrətrɪ/ | n. | It refers to a person who is employed to do office work, such as typing letters, answering phone calls, and arranging meetings. 秘书 |
| instead | /ɪnˈsted/ | ad. | in place of, or as an alternative to 代替 |
| personally | /ˈpɜːsənəlɪ/ | ad. | If you do something personally, you do it yourself rather than letting someone else do it. 亲自 |
| come over | | | If someone comes over to your house or another place, they visit you there. 拜访 |

### Activity 1  Extensive Listening

Listen to the conversation and decide whether the following statements are true (T) or false (F).

1. Mr. Black works in ABC Company.                                    (    )
2. Mr. Xia greets Mr. Black at the airport.                           (    )
3. Mr. Smith will see Mr. Black at the office.                        (    )

### Activity 2  Intensive Listening

#### Task 1 ▶

Listen to the conversation again and answer the following questions.

1. What does Xia Yu do?
2. Who is Mr. Smith?
3. Where will Mr. Black and Mr. Smith meet?

## Task 2

Listen to the conversation again and fill in the blanks with no more than three words.

A: Excuse me, but are you Mr. Black from ABC _____?

B: Yes. I'm John Black.

A: I've heard a lot about you. I'm Xia Yu, the _____ of the _____ Mr. Smith.

B: How do you do? Mr. Xia. Glad to meet you.

A: How do you do? Mr. Black. I'm here to meet you _____ Mr. Smith. He asked me to say hello to you. He is sorry he can't _____ to meet you _____.

B: It doesn't matter at all. It's very kind of you to have come.

A: My pleasure. Mr. Smith will come to meet you later at the _____.

## Activity 3  Speaking

### Language Bank

Suppose your superior has made an appointment to welcome a foreign client at the airport, but something urgent has interrupted the original plan. You have to represent him to wait for the client at the airport. When you're receiving a client at the airport on behalf of your superior, you'd better explain why your superior didn't come here and express your gratitude to clients. Here are some common expressions that might help you.

**Greeting clients on behalf of your superior:**

×××, I'm here to meet you on behalf of ×××.

Good morning, ×××. I represent my manager to pick you up. He's sorry he can't come here to meet you.

On behalf of my manager ×××, I'd like to welcome you to our city.

**Making explanations:**

××× said he's sorry but he has a very urgent task.

××× was unexpectedly tied up this morning.

××× is having a meeting now.

**Accepting explanations:**

Thank you for meeting me here.

Thank you for picking me up.

That's all right.

It doesn't matter at all.

**Appreciating clients' understanding:**

Thanks for your understanding.

I really appreciate your understanding.

That's very kind of you.

Use the expressions above. Create your own business conversation and practice it with your partner.

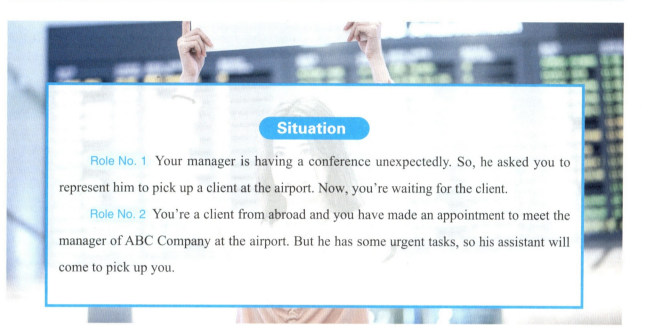

**Situation**

Role No. 1  Your manager is having a conference unexpectedly. So, he asked you to represent him to pick up a client at the airport. Now, you're waiting for the client.

Role No. 2  You're a client from abroad and you have made an appointment to meet the manager of ABC Company at the airport. But he has some urgent tasks, so his assistant will come to pick up you.

## Part III  Pick up Clients at the Airport (2)

Steven is waiting at the airport to greet his client, Kars. Will Steven finally pick up Kars and break the ice during their way to the office?

### Words and Expressions

| | | | |
|---|---|---|---|
| handling | /ˈhændlɪŋ/ | n. | the management of someone or something 处理 |
| counter | /ˈkaʊntə(r)/ | n. | In a place such as a shop or café, a counter is a long narrow table or flat surface at which customers are served. 柜台 |
| compensation | /ˌkɒmpenˈseɪʃn/ | n. | It's the money that someone who has experienced loss or suffering claims from the person or organization responsible, or from the state. 补偿金 |
| latest | /ˈleɪtɪst/ | a. | You can use latest to describe something that is very new and modern and is better than older things of a similar kind. 最新的 |
| model | /ˈmɒdl/ | n. | A particular model of a machine is a particular version of it. 型号 |

## Activity 1   Extensive Watching

Watch a short video and answer the following questions.

1. How was the client's trip?
2. Where is the client from?
3. What does the space needle look like?

## Activity 2   Intensive Watching

### Task 1

Watch the video again and choose the correct answers.

1. How often does the client go for a trip?

   A. Two times a year.　　　　　　　　B. Two or three times a year.

   C. More than three times a year.　　　D. Three times a year.

2. How long will it take from Steven's office to the airport?

   A. Around 20 minutes.　　　　　　　B. About 30 minutes.

   C. Less than 14 minutes.　　　　　　D. Over 40 minutes.

## Task 2

Watch the video again and fill in the blanks.

A: Hi, I'm Kars Tessmann.

B: Hi, I'm Steven Baker from Tech Solutions. Welcome to Seattle. So, how was your trip?

B: Not too bad, thanks. But one of my bags was _____ during the flight.

A: Oh, dear. Did you report it at _____?

B: Yes, I did. The airline will contact me next week to offer some _____.

A: Oh, good. Can I help you with your bag?

B: Yes, please. It's a bit heavy.

A: No problem. My car is this way. So, do you travel a lot?

B: Yes, about two or three times a year. I like travelling.

A: Me, too.

B: I'd like to travel more often but I'm always busy.

A: Ah, there is my car.

B: It's nice and _____ today. Is the weather usually like this in Seattle?

A: No, it's usually much _____ than this. You're very lucky. How was the weather in England?

B: It was pretty rainy.

A: I've heard it rains a lot in England.

B: Yes, it does.

A: Ah, here we are.

B: Nice car. Is that the _____?

A: Yes, it's this year's _____.

B: Thank you. How far is your office from here?

A: Oh, about 20 minutes.

B: Ah, not too far. So, what's there to do in Seattle?

A: Well, we've lots of parks, restaurants and markets. And there's the famous space needle.

B: What's that?

A: It's a tall building looks like a _____. Many tourists come to visit it.

B: Ah, I think I know the one you are talking about. I've seen it on TV.

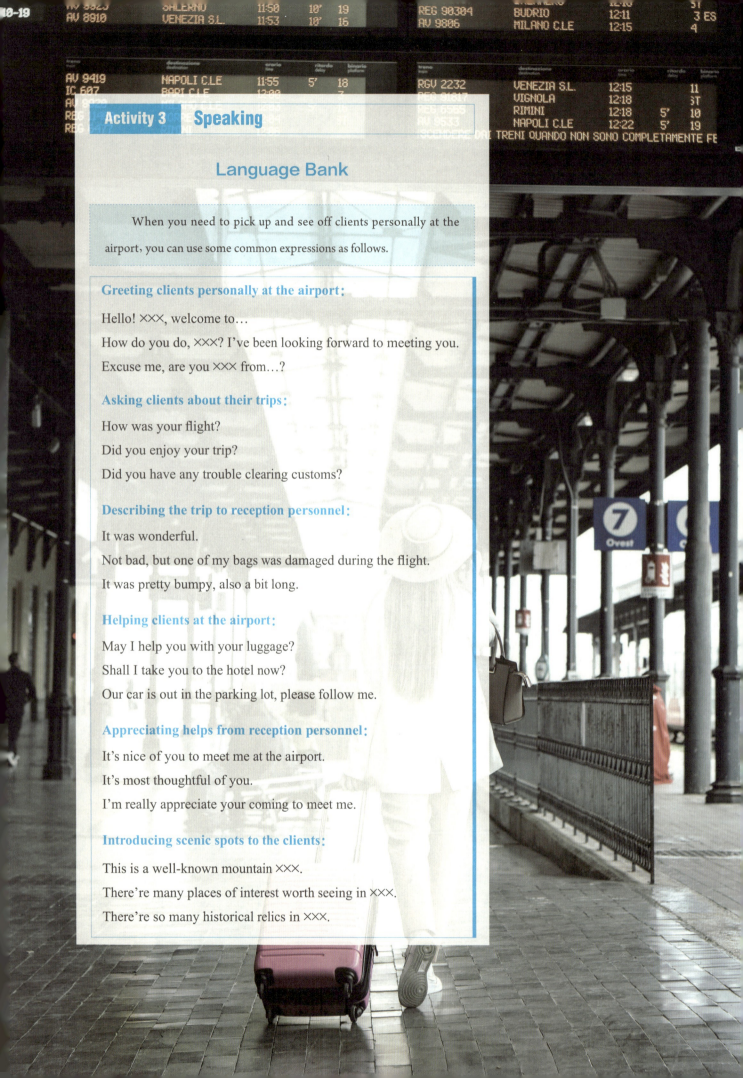

**Activity 3　Speaking**

## Language Bank

When you need to pick up and see off clients personally at the airport, you can use some common expressions as follows.

### Greeting clients personally at the airport:

Hello! ×××, welcome to…

How do you do, ×××? I've been looking forward to meeting you.

Excuse me, are you ××× from…?

### Asking clients about their trips:

How was your flight?

Did you enjoy your trip?

Did you have any trouble clearing customs?

### Describing the trip to reception personnel:

It was wonderful.

Not bad, but one of my bags was damaged during the flight.

It was pretty bumpy, also a bit long.

### Helping clients at the airport:

May I help you with your luggage?

Shall I take you to the hotel now?

Our car is out in the parking lot, please follow me.

### Appreciating helps from reception personnel:

It's nice of you to meet me at the airport.

It's most thoughtful of you.

I'm really appreciate your coming to meet me.

### Introducing scenic spots to the clients:

This is a well-known mountain ×××.

There're many places of interest worth seeing in ×××.

There're so many historical relics in ×××.

## Task 1 ▶

Use the expressions you've just learned as prompts and watch the video again. Then practice the conversation with your partner.

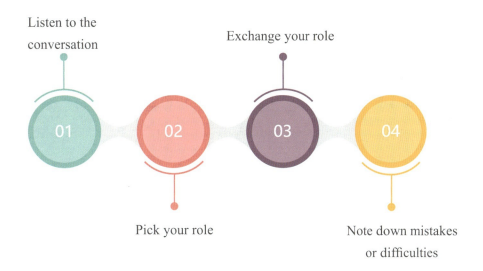

01 Listen to the conversation
02 Pick your role
03 Exchange your role
04 Note down mistakes or difficulties

## Task 2 ▶

Use the expressions above. Create your own business conversation and practice it with your group members.

**Situation**

You are a manager from ABC Company. Now, you are waiting for your business associate at the airport. Besides, as it's his first time to come here, you'd better introduce the city to him.

# Part IV  Receive Clients at the Office

In this part, you will watch a short video about conversations between two native speakers. In the video, they are making a small talk. This part consists of 3 tasks. After each watching and listening task, some useful language points will be discussed and you might use them in the following speaking task.

## Words and Expressions

| eventful | /ɪˈventfl/ | a. | full of events or incidents 多事的 |
| legroom | /ˈlegrʊm/ | n. | the amount of space, especially in a car or other vehicle, that is available in front of your legs（在车辆等座位前）供伸腿的空间 |
| location | /ləʊˈkeɪʃn/ | n. | the place where something happens or is situated 地点 |
| member | /ˈmembə(r)/ | n. | one of the people, animals, or things belonging to that group（某群体的）成员 |
| recommendation | /ˌrekəmenˈdeɪʃn/ | n. | the suggestion that someone should have or use it because it is good 推荐 |
| exhausted | /ɪgˈzɔːstɪd/ | a. | drained of energy or effectiveness; extremely tired; completely exhausted 筋疲力尽的 |
| starving | /ˈstɑːvɪŋ/ | a. | the act of depriving of food or subjecting to famine 饥饿的 |
| in person | | | in the flesh; without involving anyone else 亲自 |
| Poland | /ˈpəʊlənd/ | n. | a republic in central Europe 波兰 |
| Warsaw | /ˈwɔːsɔː/ | n. | the capital and largest city of Poland; located in central Poland 华沙（波兰首都） |

## Activity 1  Extensive Watching

Watch a short video and answer the following questions.

1. Who is Mark?
2. Has the client been to Poland before?
3. What will they do next?

Unit 6 | Receiving Clients  141

## Activity 2    Intensive Watching

 *Task 1*

Watch the video again and choose the correct answers.

1. How did Mark come to the office?
   A. By bus.    B. By car.    C. By taxi.    D. On foot.
2. How did Mark take his coffee?
   A. Just black.    B. By sugar.    C. By milk.    D. By salt.

 *Task 2*

Watch the video again and fill in the blanks.

A: Hello, you must be Mark. Nice to finally meet you in _____.

B: My pleasure. Nice to meet you too after all those phone calls.

A: Was the driver there to meet you at the airport?

B: Yes, he was. Thanks for arranging this.

A: That is the least I could do. How was your flight?

B: Long but _____, thanks. I missed the _____ but I managed to get some sleep.

A: Good to hear that. How do you like our new office?

B: Very bright and _____. Have you been in this location long?

A: W moved in others building two months ago, we've rapidly _____ last year.

B: How many people do you employ?

A: Currently, we have 30 people. I'll take you around to meet a few members of the team. They are waiting to meet you. Shall I get you something to drink?

B: A cup of coffee would be great.

A: How do you take it? Sugar? Milk?

B: Just black, thanks.

A: Have you been to Poland before?

B: Just once in Warsaw, but only for two days. I have more _____ afternoons and I was wondering if you have some _____ for me for places to see here.

A: Sure, no problem. It is 30 minutes drive to go to the sea, or forest, or city centre. You must be _____ now. After the meeting, I'll take you to your hotel where you can rest.

B: What are the plans for the evening?

A: I will pick you up at 8:00 and we are going for company dinner to a nice restaurant. I'm sure they have _____ there.

B: That's great. I am _____. It's been some time since lunch.

A: So, let's get down to business. Shall we?

B: Let's meet other _____ of the team after you.

## Activity 3  Speaking

### Language Bank

When you receive clients who just get off a plane at your office, small talk should focus on their flight, the itineraries（行程）as well as city introduction. You can use some common expressions as follows.

**Making clients feel welcome:**

I've long been looking forward to meeting you.

Nice to finally meet you in person.

Nice to meet you after all those phone calls.

Shall I get you something to drink?

Please make yourself feel at home.

**Introducing itineraries to clients:**

I'll take you around to meet a few members of the team.

After the meeting, I'll take you to your hotel where you can rest.

I will pick you up at 8:00 and we are going for company dinner to a nice restaurant.

**Complimenting the office:**

Your office is bright and airy.

The view is amazing outside your office window.

What a nice-decorated office!

**Saying goodbye to clients:**

It's a big pity you are leaving so soon.

I shall be looking forward to your visit again.

Wish you a pleasant journey, good luck.

Have a nice trip.

**Appreciating receptions of the company:**

Thanks for arranging this.

Thank you for everything you've done for me.

Thank you for your hospitality.

Thank you again for your consideration during my stay here.

## Task 1 ▶

Use the expressions you've just learned to complete the following conversation. Then practice it with your partner.

A: Hello, Mr. Green. I've _____ been looking forward to meeting you. Nice to meet you after all those _____.

B: Nice to _____ meet you _____. What a _____ office. The view is _____ outside your office window.

A: Thank you, Mr. Green. How was your flight?

B: It's long but comfortable.

A: That's _____. I will take you around to meet my colleagues. Then we will have a welcome dinner together at a local restaurant. I'm _____ you will enjoy it. After dinner, my secretary Tom will drive you around this city to see the night view.

B: Thank you for _____ this.

…

A: How times flies. It's a big _____ you are leaving so soon.

B: Thank you again for your _____ during my stay here.

## Task 2 ▶

Use the expressions above. Create your own business conversation and practice it with your group members.

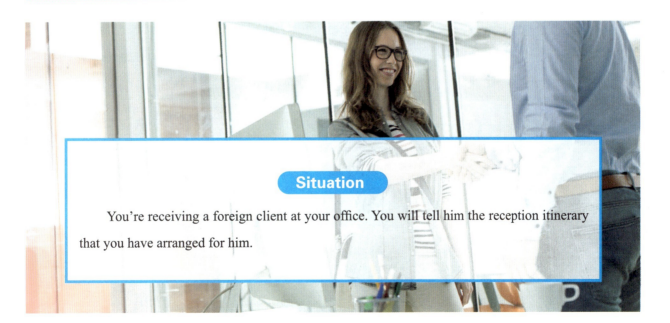

**Situation**

You're receiving a foreign client at your office. You will tell him the reception itinerary that you have arranged for him.

# Project-based Task

## Objectives

- Arrange reception plans, including pick up and office receptions.
- Assign your staff to pick up a client at the airport.
- Go to the airport to pick up another client by yourself.
- Receive clients at your office. Tell them about the reception itinerary.

## Task Background

Mary has invited some foreign clients to visit her company for cooperation. But because of the time arrangement, she can't greet the first foreign guest in person. So, in the morning, Mary assigns her staff to pick up the first client at the airport on behalf of her. And she will pick up another client later by herself. After the pick-up, Mary will greet all clients at her office in the afternoon.

## Procedures

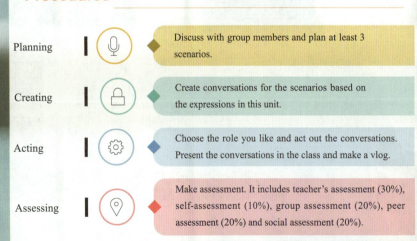

**Planning** — Discuss with group members and plan at least 3 scenarios.

**Creating** — Create conversations for the scenarios based on the expressions in this unit.

**Acting** — Choose the role you like and act out the conversations. Present the conversations in the class and make a vlog.

**Assessing** — Make assessment. It includes teacher's assessment (30%), self-assessment (10%), group assessment (20%), peer assessment (20%) and social assessment (20%).

Unit 6 | Receiving Clients

## Possible Scenarios

### Scenario 1

Mary is the manager of ABC Company. She has invited some foreign clients to visit her company. Now, she is assigning her secretary Bob to pick up one of the clients at the airport.

Role No. 1  Mary: Assign Bob to pick up a client; give him detailed information about the flight.

Role No. 2  Bob: Enquire the detailed information about the flight and the client.

…

### Scenario 2

After assigning the task, Mary and her secretary Bob go to the airport respectively. They're waiting for their clients.

Role No. 1  Mary: Pick up client A; greet him and ask about his trip.

Role No. 2  Bob: Pick up client B; greet him; explain why Mary didn't come, and introduce scenic spots to him.

Role No. 3  Client A: Chat with Mary.

Role No. 4  Client B: Feel confused why Mary didn't keep their appointment; want to know more about this city, especially the scenic spots.

…

### Scenario 3

Mary receives clients at her office. She greets them, and tells them today's reception itinerary including meeting room, dinner and night view touring, etc. And say goodbye to them at last.

Role No. 1  Mary: Receive clients; make small talk, and tell them about the reception itinerary. Say goodbye to them after the reception.

Role No. 2  Client A: Make small talk.

Role No. 3  Client B: Make small talk.

Role No. 4  Bob: Accompany the client.

Requirements:

- All group members are required to take part in the project.
- Use the expressions you have learned in this unit as many as possible.

# Self-assessment Checklist

Now, it's time for you to review your performance after learning this unit. Carry out a self-assessment by checking the following table.

| Items | Ratings | | | |
|---|---|---|---|---|
| | A | B | C | D |
| **Listening Skills** — I can understand people's relationship. | | | | |
| I can get arrangement information. | | | | |
| I can understand assigning pick-up tasks. | | | | |
| I can catch the information about making explanations. | | | | |
| I can understand descriptions about journeys. | | | | |
| I can understand help from reception personnel. | | | | |
| I can understand reception itineraries. | | | | |
| I can catch small talk information from clients. | | | | |
| **Speaking Skills** — I can describe people's relationship. | | | | |
| I can take tasks from superiors. | | | | |
| I can make explanations to clients for my superiors. | | | | |
| I can appreciate client's understanding. | | | | |
| I can ask clients about their trips. | | | | |
| I can help clients at the airport. | | | | |
| I can introduce scenic spots to clients. | | | | |
| I can introduce reception itineraries to clients. | | | | |
| **Professional Skills** — I can arrange my subordinates to receive clients at the airport. | | | | |
| I can pick up clients on behalf of my superiors. | | | | |
| I can pick up clients and introduce scenic spots to them. | | | | |
| I can receive clients at my office and make them feel at home. | | | | |

A: Basically agree

B: Agree

C: Strongly agree

D: Disagree

Unit 7

Showing Clients Around the Company

## Overview

Doing business means building economic relationships with others. So, when visitors like new clients or new colleagues arrive at the company's reception and want to know more about your company, you need to take the chance to provide professional assistance. For example, you might want to show visitors around the company and introduce them to the working environment, company facilities, new products, etc. Therefore, in this unit, we will learn **how to welcome visitors, accompany visitors while waiting, show them around offices and introduce products**. Now let us start our business journey!

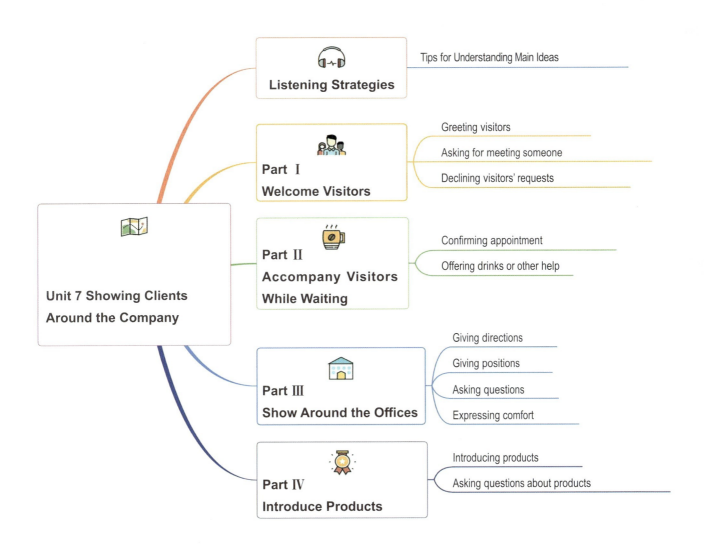

# Listening Strategies

## Understanding Main Ideas

It's essential to catch the main ideas when doing conversational listening exercise. In these conversations, however, the speed is very fast and the contents might be various. So, how can we grasp main ideas of each conversation?

### Tips for Understanding Main Ideas

In general, there will be one or two sentences as the *topic sentence* in each conversation or speech. It's a common rule no matter in a reading exam or a listening exam. Therefore, the topic sentence is the key to succeed. It's not necessary to get the idea of every sentence in the conversation, just try to figure out the meaning of the topic sentence.

The topic sentence often shows up at the beginning of a conversation to *summarize the main ideas* or *provide clues* for the following content. It's usually the first, second or the last sentence of a long conversation. Sometimes, the first question of the listening exercise might target at the beginning of the conversation. And the last question might point to the end of it. So, practice your note-taking skills and pay attention to the key information like *who*, *when*, *where*, *what*, *why* and *how*. This could help you find out the main ideas and get answers quickly.

## Task

Listen to the conversation and fill in the blanks.

### Conversation 1

A: We are proud and honored to have every guest to _____ our company.

B: Thank you very much.

A: I hope you can get a _____ of what our business is through my introduction.

B: Okay.

A: Our company was established in 1890. We specialized in manufacturing genes and exporting them to all over the world. The _____ product was named by the founders' name.

B: Could I ask what the turnover was _____?

A: Sure. It's about ten million dollars last year. And our business is still _____ steadily.

B: Your company really has strength.

### Conversation 2

A: Good morning, Ms. Bennett. Do _____. Welcome. It's nice to see you again.

B: And you. I've been very much looking forward to this visit.

A: So have we. May I take your _____?

B: Certainly. Here you are.

A: Please have a seat and make yourself comfortable. I'll tell Mr. Jenson you're here. Would you like something to drink?

B: Yes, I wouldn't mind a _____ drink if at all possible.

…

A: You're welcome. Did you have any _____ finding the way?

B: No, the directions you sent me were very clear and there was hardly any _____ on the road.

A: Excellent. How's Mr. Samuels?

B: He's very well. He _____ his regards.

### Conversation 3

A: It's me who will _____ you to visit our company today. First of all, I want to extend my _____ welcome to all of you on behalf of the company.

B: Thank you.

A: This is our office block. We have all the administrative departments _____.

B: What's that building opposite us?

A: That's the warehouse where the larger items of instruments are stored.

B: If I order an apparatus, how long would I wait for the delivery made to our company?

A: Sorry, I'm afraid you have to ask the sales _____.

B: Okay.

A: We will visit the assembly shop next. This _____, please.

# Lead-in

## Cultural Background

In everyday business, there are many situations that someone might visit your company or factory and take a tour. He/she could be a potential client, a company manager, or an official inspection (检察官). So, when someone is coming for a company visit, you need to be fully prepared and get it done well. What's more, showing a visitor around gives you a good opportunity to make a great first impression on your visitor. By welcoming a visitor with warmly hearts and introducing your workplace to him/her clearly and politely, you can build a nice starter for your business relationship between your company and your visitor's. So, first of all, make sure you've researched the visitor you're expecting, understood his or her visiting purpose so that you won't be ill-prepared (准备不足的；措手不及的). When the visitor arrives, give warmly hand-shakes and welcome. Then during the company tour, pay attention to the visitor's interests and answer his/her questions clearly. Don't forget to say goodbye to the visitor when it's finished.

### Task 1

Read the above passage and answer the following questions.

1. What kind of people might visit your company?
2. Why is it important to show visitors around the company?

### Task 2

Think about the following questions and discuss in small groups.

1. What do you need to do when showing clients around the company?
2. What do you need to do after showing clients around the company?

# Warm-up

## ◉ Task ▶

If you're going to show someone around your company, what might be the procedures? Discuss with your group members first. Then take a look at some possible steps in the following boxes and put them in a logical order.

| Lead to the factory | Say goodbye |
| Welcome | Arrive at the company |
| Waiting at the office | Lead to the office |

Step 1_____  Step 2_____  Step 3_____

Step 4_____  Step 5_____  Step 6_____

Unit 7 | Showing Clients Around the Company   155

 Business Communication

## Part I  Welcome Visitors

In this part, you will hear a business conversation between two native speakers. They introduce themselves and talk about visiting purpose in the conversation. This part consists of 3 activities. After each listening task, some useful language points will be discussed and you might use them in the following speaking task.

### Words and Expressions

| unfortunately | /ʌnˈfɔːtʃənətlɪ/ | ad. | by bad luck 不幸地；遗憾地 |
| reach | /riːtʃ/ | v. | If you try to reach someone, you try to contact them, usually by telephone. (通过电话)联系上(某人) |
| as usual | | | in the usual manner 像往常一样；照例 |
| in advance | | | situated ahead or going before; ahead of time 预先；提前 |

### Activity 1  Extensive Listening

Listen to the conversation and decide whether the following statements are true (T) or false (F).

1. Mr. Smith is asking to meet Mr. Wang.                                     (     )
2. Mr. Wang was away this afternoon.                                         (     )
3. Mr. Smith should make an appointment first.                               (     )

## Activity 2  Intensive Listening

### Task 1

Listen to the conversation and answer the following questions.

1. When will Mr. Wang come back?
2. How can Mr. Smith reach Mr. Wang?
3. Have the two speakers met before?

### Task 2

Listen to the conversation again and fill in the blanks with no more than three words.

A: Good morning.

B: Good morning, Mr. Smith. I haven't seen you for a _____. How are you?

A: Fine, thanks. And you?

B: Busy _____.

A: I want to meet Mr. Wang. I have something _____ to talk about.

B: _____, he was _____ this morning.

A: Do you know when he will come back?

B: He won't be back till _____.

A: I can't wait that long. I should make an appointment _____.

B: You can try to reach him by _____.

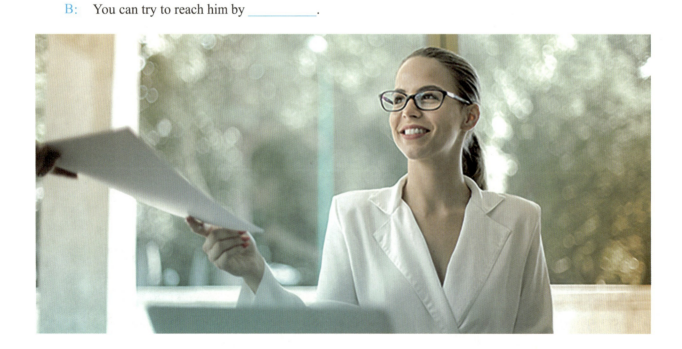

## Activity 3 | Speaking

## Language Bank

When a visiting client arrives at the company, you need to kindly greet him/her first and confirm his/her appointment. If the person he/she asks to see isn't around, you could express sorry and decline their request. Here are some common expressions you might use.

### Greeting visitors:

Good morning/afternoon/evening.

I haven't seen you for a long while.

How are you? /How have you been? /How's it going?

### Asking for meeting someone:

I want to meet ×××.

I have something important to talk to ×××.

### Declining visitors' requests:

Unfortunately, ××× was away this morning/this afternoon/at the moment.

He won't be back until…

He will be back until…

You can try to reach him by phone/e-mails.

(Perhaps) you should make an appointment in advance.

Use the expressions above. Create your own business conversation and practice it with your partner.

**Situation**

Role No. 1  You're a client and want to see the manager of ××× Company.

Role No. 2  You're the manager's assistant and your boss is not at the company right now.

# Part II  Accompany Visitors While Waiting

In this part, you will hear a business conversation between two native speakers. The visitor arrives early and she decides to wait for a while. This part consists of 3 activities. After each listening task, some useful language points will be discussed and you might use them in the following speaking task.

| Words and Expressions | | | |
|---|---|---|---|
| guest | /gest/ | n. | someone who is visiting you or is at an event because you have invited them 客人, 宾客; 顾客 |
| profile | /ˈprəʊfaɪl/ | n. | an analysis (often in graphical form) representing the extent to which something exhibits various characteristics 简介; 概况 |

## Activity 1  Extensive Listening

Listen to the conversation and decide whether the following statements are true (T) or false (F).

1. The visitor, Cindy is here to meet Mr. Thomson.     (     )
2. The visitor, Cindy has arrived earlier.     (     )
3. The secretary gave Cindy a cup of black coffee with sugar.     (     )
4. Mr. Thomson is not at the Pertamina Office right now.     (     )

## Activity 2  Intensive Listening

### Task 1

Listen to the conversation again and answer the following questions.

1. Did Cindy make an appointment in advance?
2. When will Mr. Thomson meet the visitor?
3. What did the secretary offer to the visitor while waiting?

## Task 2

*Listen to the conversation again and fill in the blanks with no more than three words.*

Secretary: Good morning and welcome to Pertamina Office.

Visitor: Good morning. My name is Cindy and I want to _____ the HRD Manager, Mr. Thomson.

Secretary: Nice to meet you. I'm Fiona, Mr. Thomson's _____ and we talked on the phone _____.

Visitor: Oh, Fiona. Nice to meet you, too.

Secretary: Please come in and have a seat.

Visitor: Thank you. Is Mr. Thomson here?

Secretary: Yes, he is. Based on our conversation yesterday, he will meet you at 10 and now he is with _____. Do you mind waiting?

Visitor: No problem. I know that I come much earlier.

Secretary: What do you want to drink, tea or coffee?

Visitor: Black coffee, please.

Secretary: Here is your coffee without sugar.

Visitor: Thank you.

Secretary: While waiting, you can read the _____ or the newspaper.

Visitor: By the way, do you have company profile that I can read?

Secretary: Here you are.

### Activity 3  Speaking

## Language Bank

Usually, when visitors with an appointment show up, you need to confirm their information and show hospitality by offering drinks or making small talks to keep them company while waiting. Here are some common expressions you might want to use.

**Confirming appointment:**

I'm ××× (name), ××× (job title). We talked on the phone/over e-mail/… yesterday/last time.

Based on our conversation yesterday, he will meet you at ××× (time).

**Offering drinks or other help:**

Please come in and have a seat.

What do you want to drink, tea or coffee?

How would you like your coffee?

He is with another guest. Do you mind waiting?

May I take your coat?

While waiting, you can read the magazine/newspaper/company profile…

Use the expressions above. Create your own business conversation and practice it with your partner.

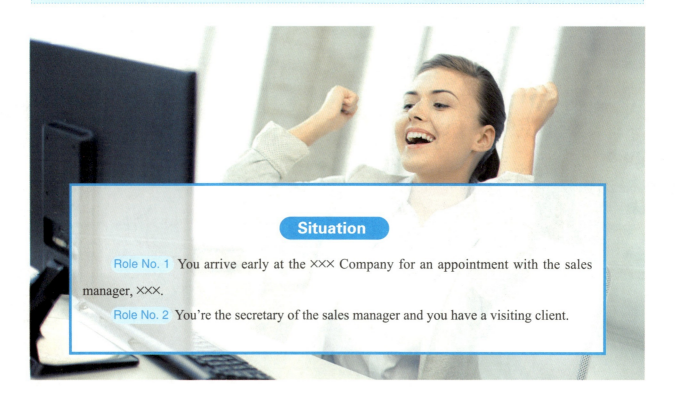

### Situation

**Role No. 1** You arrive early at the ××× Company for an appointment with the sales manager, ×××.

**Role No. 2** You're the secretary of the sales manager and you have a visiting client.

# Part III  Show Around Offices

It's Maria's first day at QPG. She is waiting for her manager, Paul. After a short and nice chat with the receptionist, Maria is going to walk with Paul and get to know about her future workplace better. Can Maria remember all those things that Paul tells her during the quick company-guided tour?

| **Words and Expressions** | | | |
|---|---|---|---|
| scanner | /ˈskænə(r)/ | n. | a machine which is used to examine, identify, or record things, for example by using a beam of light, sound, or X-rays 扫描仪；扫描器；光电子扫描装置 |
| corridor | /ˈkɒrɪdɔː(r)/ | n. | a long passage in a building, with doors and rooms on one or both sides 走廊 |
| administrative | /ədˈmɪnɪstrətɪv/ | a. | Administrative work involves organizing and supervising an organization or institution. 行政的；管理的 |
| induction | /ɪnˈdʌkʃn/ | n. | a procedure or ceremony for introducing someone to a new job, organization, or way of life 入门培训；就职仪式 |
| stationery | /ˈsteɪʃənrɪ/ | n. | paper, envelopes, and other materials or equipment used for writing 文具；信纸 |
| cupboard | /ˈkʌbəd/ | n. | a piece of furniture that has one or two doors, usually contains shelves, and is used to store things 碗柜；食橱 |
| folder | /ˈfəʊldə(r)/ | n. | a thin piece of cardboard in which you can keep loose papers 活页夹；文件夹 |
| stapler | /ˈsteɪplə(r)/ | n. | a device used for putting staples into sheets of paper 订书机 |
| anonymous | /əˈnɒnɪməs/ | a. | If you remain anonymous when you do something, you do not let people know that you were the person who did it. 匿名的，无名的 |

## Activity 1   Extensive Watching

Watch a short video and answer the following questions.

1. Where does the conversation take place?
2. Whose security pass isn't working?
3. Does Paul introduce any colleagues to Maria?

## Activity 2  Intensive Watching

### Task 1

Watch the video again and choose the correct answers.

1. Where did Maria get her security pass?

   A. Reception desk.　　B. Coffee shop.　　C. Induction.　　D. HR's meeting room.

2. Which place did Paul NOT show Maria around in the company tour today?

   A. HR's meeting room.　　　　　　　　B. Warehouse.

   C. Finance departments.　　　　　　　D. Sales and marketing departments.

### Task 2

Watch the video again and fill in the blanks.

A: So, first things first, did you get your security pass at the _____?

B: This?

A: Yes, that's it. Hold it in front of the scanner, wave it about in front of the scanner. Strange… Can I try? Right, we'll use mine. I'll take this. I'll call facilities later. Okay, this is your office here, and my office is opposite yours, right here. If we go to the end of this _____, this room is HR's meeting room. We don't have many meeting rooms in the building, so other departments sometimes share it, too.

B: Is this where I had my _____?

A: That's right. And that door over there leads to the stairs to customer services, the finance departments, sales and marketing and some other _____. But if we go this way first, I'll show you where to find some administrative things. So, these are our stationery cupboards. You'll find everything you need in here. Pens, paper, folders, staplers, hole punches… the lots.

B: Can I just help myself?

A: Yes, anything you need.

B: Right.

A: And here are all our HR and _____ forms. We still use hard copies for training courses.

B: Oh, right.

A: Well, you know, feedback forms aren't anonymous if people have to email them, aren't they?

B: No, of course.

Unit 7 | Showing Clients Around the Company

A: And these are our _____ copiers. Something wrong here… Anyway, never mind about that. Do I need to show you anything else?

B: Uh, toilets.

A: Oh, yes. if you go to the end of this corridor, past the _____ doors, turn right, the ladies are on your left.

B: Okay.

A: It can feel like a maze at first. You'll be fine in a few days. Shall I show you some other departments? I could introduce you to some colleagues if they're here.

B: Yes. That would be good. Thank you.

…

A: And this is our corridor again.

B: Oh yes. Well, thanks for the _____.

A: Yes, it's a shame. Anna wasn't in our office, but at least you know where it is now anyway. Let's have a chat about the rest of your day.

## Activity 3  Speaking

## Language Bank

During a company tour with visitors, you can use some common expressions as follows to introduce your workplace.

**Giving directions:**

If we/you go to the end of this ×××, this room is…

That door over there leads to the starts to…

But if we go this way first, I'll show you where to…

Pass the ×××.

Turn right/left.

The ××× is/are on your right/left.

**Giving positions:**

This is the ××× here.

The ××× is opposite/beside/in front of ×××, right here.

And this is our ××× again.

**Asking questions:**

Can I just help myself?

Shall I show you some other departments?

Is this where I had…?

**Expressing comfort (new employee):**

You'll find everything you need here.

You'll be fine in a few days.

At least you know where it is now anyway.

Feel free to ask questions.

## Task 1

Use the expressions you've just learned as prompts and watch the video again. Then practice the conversation with your partner.

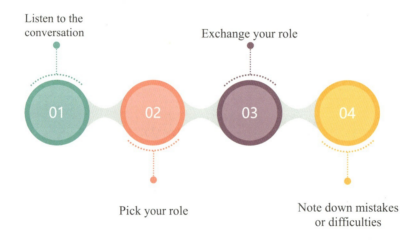

01 Listen to the conversation
02 Pick your role
03 Exchange your role
04 Note down mistakes or difficulties

## Task 2

Use the expressions above. Create your own business conversation and practice it with your group members.

**Situation**

You are the HR manager and you need to give a quick company tour to the client who visits your company for the first time.

Unit 7 | Showing Clients Around the Company   165

# Part IV  Introduce Products

In this part, you will watch a short video about conversations between some native speakers. In the video, they meet some new people and talk about some company products. This part consists of 3 tasks. After each watching and listening task, some useful language points will be discussed and you might use them in the following speaking task.

## Words and Expressions

| | | | |
|---|---|---|---|
| disturb | /dɪˈstɜːb/ | v. | If you disturb someone, you interrupt what they are doing and upset them. 打扰；妨碍 |
| advertising | /ˈædvətaɪzɪŋ/ | n. | the activity of creating advertisements and making sure people see them 广告；广告业 |
| workshop | /ˈwɜːkʃɒp/ | n. | small workplace where handcrafts or manufacturing are done 车间；研讨会；工场 |
| manufacture | /ˌmænjʊˈfæktʃə/ | v. | to manufacture something means to make it in a factory, usually in large quantities 制造，加工；生产 |
| license | /ˈlaɪsns/ | n. | a legal document giving official permission to do something 执照，许可证；特许 |
| expertise | /ˌekspɜːˈtiːz/ | n. | special skill or knowledge that is acquired by training, study, or practice 专业技能；专业知识 |
| complicated | /ˈkɒmplɪkeɪtɪd/ | a. | difficult to analyze or understand 难懂的，复杂的 |
| in house | | | work or activities are done by employees of an organization or company, rather than by workers outside the organization or company 机构内部的 |

## Activity 1    Extensive Watching

Watch a short video and answer the following questions.

1. Where does this conversation take place?
2. How many people are there in this conversation?
3. Do these speakers work in the same company?

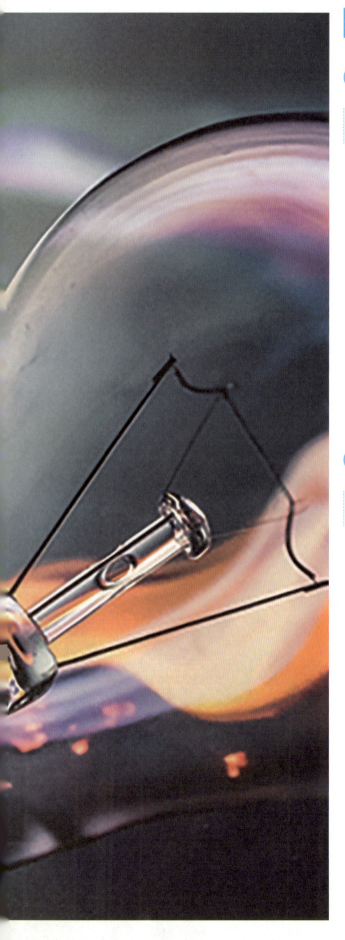

## Activity 2　Intensive Watching

### Task 1

Watch the video again and choose the correct answers.

1. What kind of company does Phil work for?
   A. Chemical Industry.
   B. Advertising Industry.
   C. Manufacturing Industry.
   D. Food Industry.

2. Who has the idea for designing the beautiful products?
   A. Derek.
   B. A young girl from a local school.
   C. A college student.
   D. Phil.

### Task 2

Watch the video again and fill in the blanks.

A: Sorry to _____ you, Derek.

B: Not at all.

A: Have you met Phil Watson, from Roy Jay Advertising?

B: No, I don't think so.

A: Phil, I'd like to introduce Derek Jones, our _____.

B: Glad to meet you.

A: This whole area is our development workshop. It's where we work on the ideas for new products and toys.

C: Who gives you the _____?

A: Most of the ideas come from inside the company.

C: Who thought of this?

A: This product here is being manufactured under _____ from a company in the States. It's not our concept, I'm afraid, but it's selling very _____. We have a very flexible position on licensing deals.

C: This looks beautiful.

A: Derek, whose idea was this? Did you think of this one?

B: No. It's quite nice, isn't it? That toy started life as a picture from a young girl from a local school. She sent it in to us. Ah, here it is.

C: How do you do your market research for a new product?

A: Good question. It depends on the products. We have our own research people _____ so we do very detailed assessments. But, of course, we buy in market research expertise when we look outside the _____ marketing. Big boss is very complicated. We're targeting both _____ and children.

C: Nice to meet you, Derek.

B: You, too. I hope you get the packaging designs _____. Big boss deserves the best.

## Activity 3  Speaking

## Language Bank

During a company tour, you might want to show visitors around your workshop and how products are made. You can use some common expressions as follows.

**Introducing products:**

This product here is being manufactured under license from…

It's (not) our…, I'm afraid.

It's selling very fast.

It's quite nice, isn't it?

That ××× started life as…

We're targeting both… and…

**Asking questions about products:**

Who gives you the ideas?

Who thought of this?

Whose idea was this?

Did you think of this one?

How do you do your market research for a new product?

## Task 1

Use the expressions you've just learned to complete the following conversation. Then practice it with your partner.

A: Nice to meet you, _____. I'm _____, the _____ of ABC Company. I'd like to show you _____.

B: Nice to meet you, too.

A: This whole area is our _____. It's where we work on _____ for _____.

B: This one looks interesting. Who gives you the _____?

B: The ideas come from _____. And this product is selling _____.

A: Okay.

B: Let me show you another _____.

## Task 2

Use the expressions above. Create your own business conversation and practice it with your group members.

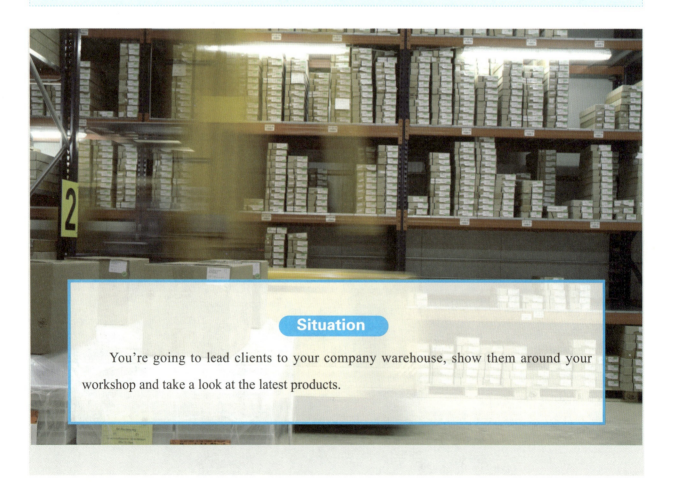

**Situation**

You're going to lead clients to your company warehouse, show them around your workshop and take a look at the latest products.

# Project-based Task

## Objectives

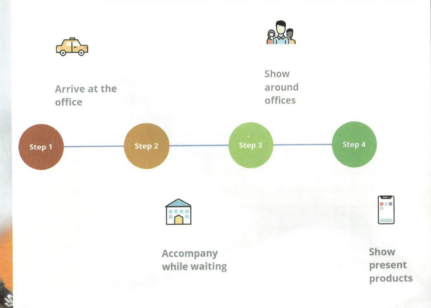

## Task Background

Sam had just arrived in this city and he can't wait to pay a visit to his old business partner, Tim, the development manager of ABC Company. Unfortunately, Tim wasn't around for the first time. Sam reached him and arranged a second visit. This time, Sam and his assistant are going to visit Tim's new workshop and have a discussion about their latest product for further cooperation.

**Procedures**

| | | |
|---|---|---|
| Planning | 🎤 | Discuss with group members and plan at least 3 scenarios. |
| Creating | 🔒 | Create conversations for the scenarios based on the expressions in this unit. |
| Acting | ⚙️ | Choose the role you like and act out the conversations. Present the conversations in the class and make a vlog. |
| Assessing | 📍 | Make assessment. It includes teacher's assessment (30%), self-assessment (10%), group assessment (20%), peer assessment (20%) and social assessment (20%). |

## Possible Scenarios

### Scenario 1

After a short rest at the hotel, Sam wants to pay a visit to Tim because his new company is just nearby. He follows the address and arrives at his office. But Tim's secretary says he is currently out of town…

Role No. 1  Sam: Ask for meeting Tim

Role No. 2  Tim's secretary: Greet Sam and his assistant

Role No. 3  Sam's assistant: Wait with Sam

### Scenario 2

This time, Sam brings along his assistant to visit Tim's office again. They arrive a bit early and Tim's still with some other guests. So, they wait for a moment outside his office.

Role No. 1  Sam: Confirm the appointment with Tim's secretary

Role No. 2  Tim's secretary: Talk to the visitors

Role No. 3  Sam's assistant: Wait with Sam

### Scenario 3

Tim greets his old business partner and leads them to see his new workplace. During the company tour, Tim introduces the latest product on the desk to Sam and his assistant.

Role No. 1  Sam: Ask Tim about his new company

Role No. 2  Tim: Introduce the company

Role No. 3  Sam's assistant: Assist Sam

Role No. 4  Tim's secretary: Assist Tim

Requirements:

- All group members are required to take part in the project.
- Use the expressions you have learned in this unit as many as possible.

# Self-assessment Checklist

Now, it's time for you to review your performance after learning this unit. Carry out a self-assessment by checking the following table.

| Items | | Ratings | | | |
|---|---|---|---|---|---|
| | | A | B | C | D |
| Listening Skills | I can understand the main ideas. | | | | |
| | I can get key information. | | | | |
| | I can understand greetings and confirmations of the appointments when I arrive at the company. | | | | |
| | I can catch the information about a business appointment. | | | | |
| | I can understand directions and positions during a company tour. | | | | |
| | I can understand expressions that are offering help. | | | | |
| | I can understand the expressions of declining a visit. | | | | |
| | I can understand the introduction of company products. | | | | |
| Speaking Skills | I can ask for the information about directions and positions. | | | | |
| | I can greet and introduce myself. | | | | |
| | I can ask for meeting someone. | | | | |
| | I can ask related questions during a company tour. | | | | |
| | I can make a business appointment. | | | | |
| | I can introduce company products. | | | | |
| | I can ask questions about company products. | | | | |
| | I can give directions and positions during a company tour. | | | | |
| Professional Skills | I can welcome visitors who arrive at the company. | | | | |
| | I can accompany visitors while they are waiting for the meeting. | | | | |
| | I can show visitors around the company and help them to know the company better. | | | | |
| | I can introduce products to visitors during a company tour. | | | | |

A: Basically agree

B: Agree

C: Strongly agree

D: Disagree

# Unit 8

## Entertaining Clients

# Overview

In order to close a deal in business, most of the time people choose to host some client appreciation or recognition events to build up a better business relationship. So, how can we make sure that the money we've spent on the client entertaining is worth every penny of it? In this unit, we will focus on the topic of entertaining business clients and learn **how to plan entertainments, invite clients for a meal or outdoor activities and bond with clients.** Now let us start our business journey!

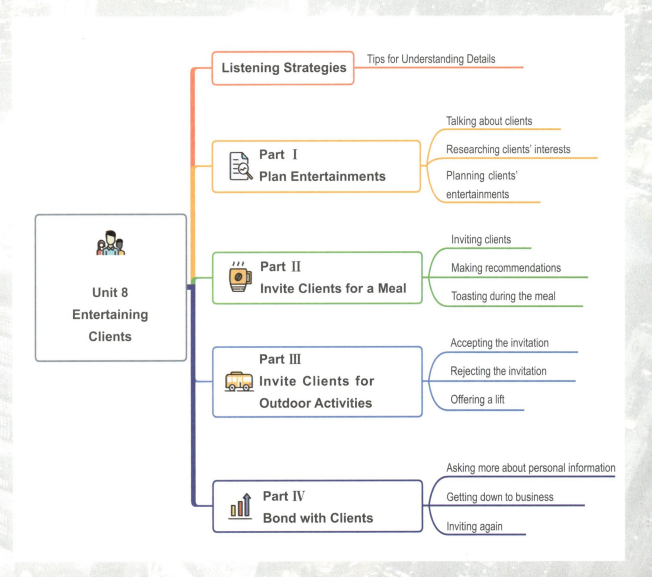

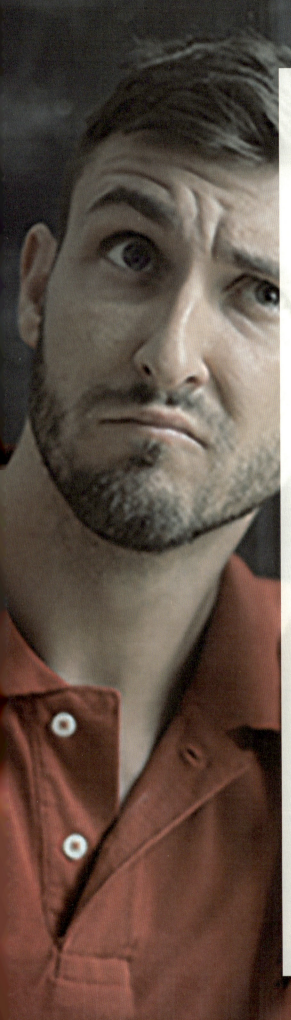

##  Listening Strategies

### Understanding Details

In most of the English listening exams, it's not enough to just understand the main ideas. Finding detailed information of each conversation is also important. They are sometimes facts or numbers that are difficult for candidates to catch during a long conversation or speech. So, how can we solve this kind of problem?

#### Tips for Understanding Details

Some listening exercises are targeted at detailed information, such as **flight numbers, phone numbers, address, time, locations, names**, etc.

In order to successfully grasp the key information while listening, the first thing is to pay attention to words that are **verbs, nouns, pronouns, adjectives, adverbs** and **numbers**. Practice the note-taking skills to write down these words the first or second time you hear the audio. You can make your own special abbreviation for some of them, like "U" for "You".

Secondly, before listening, go through the directions or questions first, underline some keywords in the statement, then make a prediction about the answers. This will help you get a rough direction of how the conversation would go. For example, in a question like "*May I offer you something to *drink, coffee, tea* or _____?*", it is obvious to assume that the blank stands for some kind of beverage. Then you can leave a mark beside to remind yourself.

Unit 8 | Entertaining Clients

Listen to the conversation and fill in the blanks.

### Conversation 1

A: Hi, Mr. Wang. Do you feel like going _____ with me?

B: Sounds _____. I haven't gone boating (划船) for some time now. And what time?

A: How about tomorrow _____?

B: Sure. Where shall I meet you?

A: At the _____ of the park.

B: Great. I look forward to meeting you.

A: See you _____.

B: See you.

### Conversation 2

B: Again, it's pleasure to work with you, Mr. Smith. Have you _____ a tour to the city yet?

A: No, I haven't. Are there any _____ destinations (目的地)?

B: I have _____ recommendations (推荐) for you. But it's a bit far from here and it takes about _____.

A: Well, I think I only have a short time for _____ afternoon.

B: If that's the case, I think you could go to the _____ garden. May I pick you up tomorrow?

A: That would be great. You are so kind.

### Conversation 3

A: Do you make machines for _____ such things?

B: Yes, we have a showroom (样品间) not far away from here, Mr. Black. Are you _____ now?

A: Yes, quite free until _____.

B: Fine. Then, shall we go right away? I have a _____ outside.

A: Have you? That's splendid (太好了; 太棒了). Just let me get my things together. I won't keep you long.

B: Take your _____, sir. I can wait.

# Lead-in

## Cultural Background

It's universal to show politeness and professionalism (专业性) when doing business, so that you can give a great impression on your clients. If you want to show true appreciation or recognition to your clients, or just simply motivate them before signing the contract, it's necessary to plan some entertaining activities. Some choose to invite clients for lunch, dinner or a golf match out of personal interests, while others invite them for large events like business party or opening ceremony. What's important is that they have to be focused, memorable, and better off customized (量身定制的), such as a dinner in a private restaurant with wine tasting or cooking demonstration. Because for business people who travel between big cities and countries, they might not remember a specific event unless it has something special. We all want our money to be spent on where it counts the most. So, make sure that your clients feel special in your entertaining events and it will do a great help for your business relationship.

### Task 1 ▶

Read the above passage and answer the following questions.

1. What is the purpose of entertaining clients?
2. What are the ways to entertain clients?

### Task 2 ▶

Think about the following questions and discuss in small groups.

1. What do you need to do before hosting a client entertaining activity?
2. What do you need to do during the client entertaining activity?

# Warm-up

## Task ▶

In your study group, interview at least 3 group mates and ask them about their preference of business entertainments. You can also add your own questions about the topic "entertaining clients". Use the class survey worksheet to note down their answers, and then share with your classmates.

| Class Survey | | | | |
|---|---|---|---|---|
| Questions | Student 1 | Student 2 | Student 3 | ... |
| If you are a client, what's your favorite entertaining activity? | | | | |
| If you are a client, what's your least favorite entertaining activity? | | | | |
| ... | | | | |
| | | | | |

# Business Communication

## Part I  Plan Entertainments

In this part, you will hear a business conversation between Don and his boss. They are planning to close a deal with the Japanese client, Sakai, who loves to play golf. This part consists of 3 activities. After each listening task, some useful language points will be discussed and you might use them in the following speaking task.

### Words and Expressions

| | | | |
|---|---|---|---|
| dealer | /ˈdiːlə(r)/ | n. | a person whose business involves buying and selling things 商人（商业）；经销商 |
| golfer | /ˈɡɒlfə(r)/ | n. | a person who plays golf for pleasure or as a profession 高尔夫球手 |

### Activity 1  Extensive Listening

Listen to the conversation and decide whether the following statements are true (T) or false (F).

1. Don already made plans for this weekend. ( )
2. Sakai is back in New York for a week. ( )
3. Sakai stays in a hotel. ( )

### Activity 2  Intensive Listening

#### Task 1

Listen to the conversation and answer the following questions.

1. Who is Sakai interested in?
2. What kind of activity will Don invite Sakai to take part in?
3. How does Sakai go back to Japan?

## Task 2

Listen to the conversation again and fill in the blanks with no more than three words.

A: Don, what are your _____ for this weekend?

B: Nothing _____. Why?

A: Sakai is back in London for a week before flying home. He still hasn't _____ which company he wants to deal with. He is interested in dealer Dan. We will have to _____. We have to close this deal. He may be free this _____. And a friend of Sakai told me he's a _____ golfer. Will you be able to offer him a _____?

B: Yes. I could _____ him at his hotel.

## Activity 3　Speaking

### Language Bank

In order to plan a special and customized entertaining activity for your clients, you need to do some preparations like doing personal research on the targeted client. Here're some expressions you might use.

**Talking about clients:**

×× is back in… (location) for… (time).
×× is arriving at…
×× may be free/have time/available this… (time).
×× still hasn't decided which company he/she wants to deal with.
×× is interested in/intends to (work with) ××.
We will have to work hard/close this deal.

**Researching clients' interests:**

A friend of ×× told me he/she is a…
I heard that ×× is into/a big fan of…

**Planning clients' entertainments:**

Will you be able to/Can you offer him/her a…?
Could you invite him/her to…?
Can you make some arrangements?

Use the expressions above. Create your own business conversation and practice it with your partner.

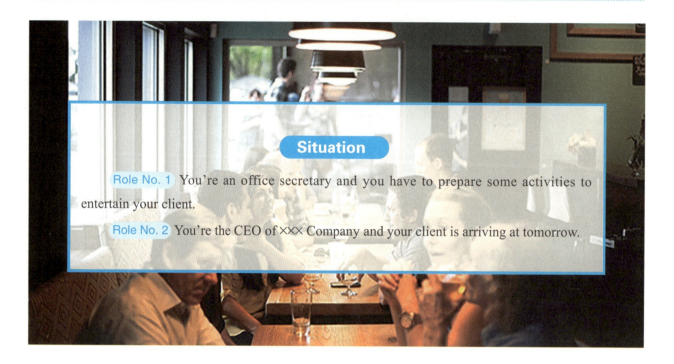

**Situation**

Role No. 1 You're an office secretary and you have to prepare some activities to entertain your client.

Role No. 2 You're the CEO of ××× Company and your client is arriving at tomorrow.

# Part II  Invite Clients for a Meal

In this part, you will listen to a conversation between Sheila, a consultant in Mumbai, and Jeremy, a British client of Sheila's company who is visiting the city. This part consists of 3 activities. After each listening task, some useful language points will be discussed and you might use them in the following speaking task.

| Words and Expressions ||||
|---|---|---|---|
| associate | /əˈsəʊsɪeɪt/ | n. | a person who is frequently in the company of another (生意或工作上的) 伙伴; 准会员; 联想 |
| pint | /paɪnt/ | n. | a unit of measurement for liquids. It is equal to 473 cubic centimeters or one eighth of a gallon 品脱 (液量单位,1英制品脱=568立方厘米,1美制品脱=473立方厘米) |
| resounding | /rɪˈzaʊndɪŋ/ | a. | You can refer to a very great success as a resounding success. 彻底的; 轰动的 |
| marvelous | /ˈmɑːvələs/ | a. | If you describe someone or something as marvelous, you are emphasizing that they are very good. 美妙的; 非凡的 |
| joint | /dʒɔɪnt/ | n. | a cheap place where people go for some form of entertainment as a joint 廉价娱乐场所 |
| draught beer | | | beer drawn from a keg 生啤酒 |

### Activity 1 — Extensive Listening

Listen to the conversation and decide whether the following statements are true (T) or false (F).

1. Sheila invited Jeremy to have some drinks and dinner with her and Tanya. ( )
2. They will meet each other at Café Blue at six. ( )
3. Tanya was late for the meeting at the café. ( )
4. Sheila and Jeremy ordered two pints of beer. ( )

### Activity 2 — Intensive Listening

#### Task 1

Listen to the conversation again and answer the following questions.

1. Who missed the meeting in the afternoon?
2. Where did they leave for after drinking beers at Café Blue?
3. How did Jeremy think of Café Blue?

## Task 2

> Listen to the conversation again and fill in the blanks with no more than three words.

A: I was wondering, Jeremy, if you would like to join my associate, Tanya, and me for _____ tonight.

B: Sounds great. Where shall we meet?

A: I was thinking Café Blue on Marine Drive First (海滨第一快道), perhaps, for a couple of drinks before we eat.

B: Excellent. Around _____ -ish?

A: Perfect.

…

B: Good evening, Sheila. I hope you haven't been waiting long.

A: Not at all. I just arrived myself.

B: Wonderful. Shall we _____?

A: Sure. This one over there with a good view. Tanya is on her way and should be joining us shortly.

B: No problem.

A: Would you like something to drink while we wait?

B: Sure. Can you _____ a good Indian beer for me?

A: The Kingfisher draught beer is particularly good.

B: Sounds great. I'll have a pint of that then.

A: Three pints of Kingfisher, please. Oh, here's Tanya, now. Let me introduce you. Tanya Roy. Jeremy Marchbanks.

B: It's great to finally meet you, Tanya.

C: It's nice to meet you too, Jeremy. I'm sorry to have missed the meeting _____.

B: Well, I'd say it was a resounding success. Wouldn't you agree, Sheila?

A: Definitely. I think we _____ a lot today. Here are the drinks now. Cheers everyone.

B: Here's to our plans and the success they'll bring.

C: Yes, here's to the deal.

A: Here, here.

…

B: That was marvelous. What a great bar.

A: Now you see why this is one of my favorite joints in the city?

C: _____.

A: Well, if everyone is done, we should be leaving soon. The dinner _____ in half an hour. And we need to beat the Mumbai traffic along the way.

B: Great. _____.

## Activity 3  Speaking

## Language Bank

Generally, people choose to invite their business partners or clients for a meal first to get to know each other better. Here are some common expressions you might want to use.

**Inviting clients:**

I was wondering if you would like to join…

Would you like to…?/Why don't you…?

Perhaps you could join us (for dinner)…

It would be great if you could join us.

I hear you like/play/enjoy/love/are keen to…

I'm a member of a very good ××× club that's not far from your hotel/place.

Would you care for a…?

How about on… (date/time)?

**Making recommendations:**

Would you like something to drink?

Can you recommend a… for me?

The… is particularly good.

Now you see why this is one of my favorite… in the city.

**Toasting during the meal:**

I'd say it was a resounding success. Wouldn't you agree?

I think we accomplished a lot today.

Here are the drinks now. Cheers (everyone).

Here's/Cheers to our… and the success they'll bring.

Here's to the deal.

Use the expressions above. Create your own business conversation and practice it with your partner.

**Situation**

Role No. 1  You are the market director and you invited your client for a business lunch.

Role No. 2  You are the client who is going to a business lunch.

# Part III  Invite Clients for Outdoor Activities

Mr. Sakai is back from his trip now. So, Don from the Bibury Systems, wants to take the opportunity and invite his client to play golf. He's learned that Mr. Sakai is keen on playing golf. How will Don arrange this client entertainment and will he succeed?

| Words and Expressions | | | |
|---|---|---|---|
| lobby | /ˈlɒbɪ/ | n. | a large entrance or reception room or area 大厅；休息室；会客室 |
| tourist site | | | a space or region whose main function is tourism and its related activities 游览地 |

### Activity 1  Extensive Watching

Watch a short video and answer the following questions.

1. Did Mr. Sakai and Don have a conversation in person?
2. Who has just finished his trip?
3. When will they meet for playing golf?

### Activity 2  Intensive Watching

#### Task 1

Watch the video again and choose the correct answers.

1. What is Mr. Sakai going to do tomorrow?

   A. Play golf with Don.

   B. Have lunch with Don.

   C. Take a flight.

   D. Visit some tourist sites.

2. When will Don come to collect Mr. Sakai?

   A. On Monday.      B. On Tuesday.

   C. On Sunday.      D. On Saturday.

## Task 2

Watch the video again and fill in the blanks.

A: Ah, Mr. Sakai. This is Don Bradley from Bibury Systems.
B: Oh, yes. Hello, Don.
A: How's your _____ going?
B: Very well, thank you. _____, but very useful.
A: I hear you play _____.
B: That's right, I do.
A: I'm a member of a very good _____ that's not far from your hotel. Would you care for a round tomorrow?
B: Thank you very much, but I have just _____ to visit some _____ tomorrow.
A: Then how about on Sunday?
B: Yes, that's fine.
A: Can I _____ you a lift? I'll come to collect you at your _____ at 10:30.
B: That's very nice of you.
A: Let's meet in the hotel _____.
B: Fine.

## Activity 3   Speaking

### Language Bank

Sometimes, people would also arrange some outdoor activities to entertain their clients. The first thing we should consider about is the clients' interests. You can use some common expressions as follows.

**Accepting the invitation:**

That's very kind/nice of you.
Sounds good.

**Rejecting the invitation:**

Thank you (very much), but I have (just) arranged to…
Unfortunately, I have another engagement but thank you for your invitation.

**Offering a lift:**

Can/May I offer you a lift?
I'll come to collect you/pick you up at… (location/time).

### Task 1

Use the expressions you've just learned as prompts and watch the video again. Then practice the conversation with your partner.

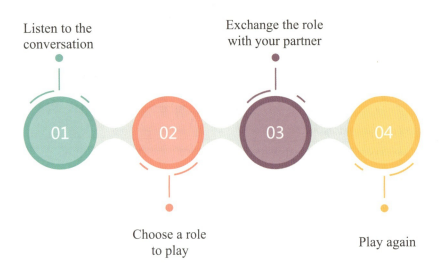

01 Listen to the conversation

02 Choose a role to play

03 Exchange the role with your partner

04 Play again

### Task 2

Use the expressions above. Create your own business conversation and practice it with your group members.

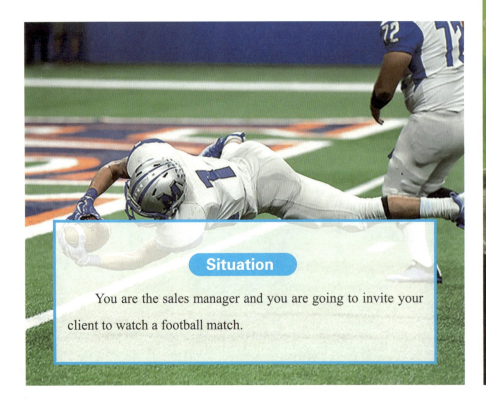

**Situation**

You are the sales manager and you are going to invite your client to watch a football match.

# Part IV  Bond with Clients

In this part, you will watch a short video about Don and his client, Mr. Sakai. After a golf game, they get to know each other better and agree to hangout again. It seems like they are becoming friends. Listen to their conversation and finish the tasks.

| Words and Expressions | | | |
|---|---|---|---|
| rival | /ˈraɪvl/ | n. | a person, business, or organization who you are competing or fighting against in the same area or for the same things 竞争对手 |
| countryside | /ˈkʌntrɪsaɪd/ | n. | land which is away from towns and cities 农村，乡下；乡下的全体居民 |
| launch | /lɔːntʃ/ | v. | If a company launches a new product, it makes it available to the public. 推出（新产品）；发行，投放市场 |

## Activity 1  Extensive Watching

Watch a short video and answer the following questions.

1. Which product does Mr. Sakai prefer?
2. Why did Don come to the UK?
3. Why does Don like living in the UK?

## Activity 2  Intensive Watching

### Task 1

Watch the video again and choose the correct answers.

1. How often does Don play golf now?

   A. Twice a week.              B. Once a week.
   C. Haven't played it for two weeks.    D. Haven't played it for three weeks.

2. When will they go to the theatre together?

   A. This evening.   B. Tomorrow afternoon.   C. Tomorrow evening.   D. Next Sunday.

## Task 2

Watch the video again and fill in the blanks.

A: How often do you _____ to play golf?

B: I like to play twice a week but neither Clive nor I have been able to play for the last three weeks because we've been too busy.

…

A: If I could just touch on business for a second.

B: Please, do.

A: Let me be open-ended. A rival of Bibury Systems is not only _____ a similar product but it's also launching it around at the same time.

B: Have you seen the rival product?

A: Yes. I've seen Dealer Dan.

B: Which _____ would you prefer?

A: Personally, I like the boss better.

…

A: Why did you come to the UK?

B: My wife is English. We lived in _____ for a while but she prefers living near her family.

A: How did you meet your wife?

B: After university, I came to Europe to have a short holiday. At least that was the plan. Within six months, I was both married and working for Bibury Systems and I'm still here.

A: You must like living in the UK then.

B: At first, I thought I would never get used to the weather, but there are lots of good things. I love the _____, and I really enjoy going to the theatre.

A: Ah, you like the theater.

B: I love the theater.

A: That's good. I was planning to go to the theater to see *Twelfth Night* (《第十二夜》，莎士比亚戏剧). Do you have any plans for tomorrow evening?

B: No, not really.

A: If you can spare the time, _____ you and your wife would care to join me.

B: Well, I'll have to check with her but it sounds like a wonderful idea. And after the play, you must let us buy you dinner _____.

…

A: See you tomorrow, Don.

B: Bye-bye.

### Activity 3  Speaking

## Language Bank

After each client entertainment, you might find yourself closer to the clients and you're bonding with them through exchanging more personal information. You might even make another arrangement. Here are some common expressions you might want to use.

**Asking more about personal information:**

How often do you manage to…?

Why did you come to…?

How did you meet your ×××?

**Getting down to business:**

If I could just touch on business for a second.

Can/May I just get down to business for a moment?

Let me be open.

**Inviting again:**

Do you have any plans for… (time)?

If you can spare the time, perhaps… would care to joint me (to the…).

After the…, you must let me/us buy you lunch/dinner… in return.

### Task 1

Use the expressions you've just learned to complete the following conversation. Then practice it with your partner.

A: Thank you for your kind tour. You must like living in the _____.

B: Well, _____. I love the _____ and also enjoy _____.

A: Really, you like _____?

B: Yes, I do.

A: That's wonderful. I always want to go to _____. Do you have _____ for tomorrow?

B: _____.

A: If you can _____, maybe you can join me.

B: Yes, _____. And after the play, you must let me _____ in return.

A: I'll see you then.

### Task 2

Use the expressions above. Create your own business conversation and practice it with your group members.

**Situation**

You take the clients for a tour in the city, and then you find out that you all like playing ping-pong. So, you plan to invite the clients again.

# Project-based Task

## Objectives

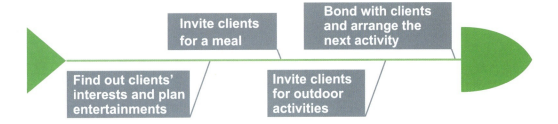

## Task Background

Alex is told by his boss that Mr. Bradly and his team are coming to the city. They have to take the chance and close the deal with him. In order to beat their competitors, Alex is going to run some background research and plan some special entertainments for Mr. Bradly and his team.

## Procedures

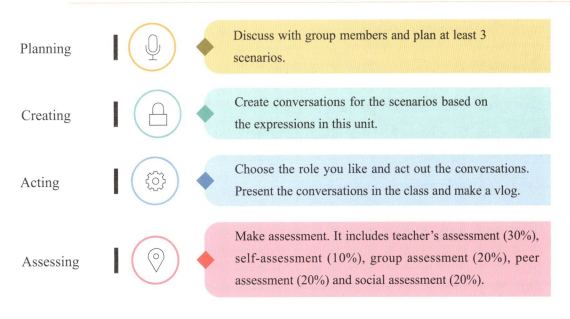

## Possible Scenarios

### ◯ Scenario 1 ▶

At the company office, Alex's boss is telling him that Mr. Bradly and his team will arrive at the airport tomorrow. They have to prepare some special events to welcome their important clients.

Role No. 1  Alex's boss: Ask Alex to plan entertainments

Role No. 2  Alex: Plan entertainments

…

### ◯ Scenario 2 ▶

After a short meeting with Mr. Bradly and his team, Alex and his boss invite them for a lunch in a nice restaurant to express their welcome and appreciation again.

Role No. 1  Alex's Boss: Invite clients to lunch

Role No. 2  Alex: Invite clients to lunch

Role No. 3  Mr. Bradly: Accept the invitation

Role No. 4  Mr. Bradly's teammate 1: Express gratitude

…

( Role No. 5  Mr. Bradly's teammate 2)

### ◯ Scenario 3 ▶

Alex and Mr. Bradly are having a great time at the lunch. They both love wine. So, Alex invites him to a wine tasting. And this time, he plans to touch on the business…

Role No. 1  Alex: Invite clients to wine tasting

Role No. 2  Mr. Bradly: Accept the invitation

Role No. 3  Mr. Bradly's teammate 1: Express gratitude

…

( Role No. 4  Mr. Bradly's teammate 2)

Requirements:

- All group members are required to take part in the project.
- Use the expressions you have learned in this unit as many as possible.

# Self-assessment Checklist

Now, it's time for you to review your performance after learning this unit. Carry out a self-assessment by checking the following table.

| Items | | Ratings | | | |
|---|---|---|---|---|---|
| | | A | B | C | D |
| Listening Skills | I can recognize the key information. | | | | |
| | I can identify parts of speech of words and phrases. | | | | |
| | I can make predictions before listening to the conversation. | | | | |
| | I can catch the information about a business event. | | | | |
| | I can understand the invitation for business events. | | | | |
| | I can understand recommendations for entertainments. | | | | |
| | I can catch the personal information during the conversation with others. | | | | |
| | I can understand the rejection of a business invitation. | | | | |
| Speaking Skills | I can ask for the information about clients' interests. | | | | |
| | I can make an invitation to business partners. | | | | |
| | I can accept the invitation from business partners. | | | | |
| | I can reject the invitation from business partners. | | | | |
| | I can offer help to our clients. | | | | |
| | I can get down to business during the entertainments. | | | | |
| | I can exchange more personal information with clients during the entertainments. | | | | |
| | I can bond with clients by inviting them out again. | | | | |
| Professional Skills | I can plan appropriate client entertainments. | | | | |
| | I can research and find out clients' interests before they arrived at the company. | | | | |
| | I can invite clients for meals and outdoor activities. | | | | |
| | I can bond with clients during the entertainments. | | | | |

A: Basically agree

B: Agree

C: Strongly agree

D: Disagree

# Unit 9

## Dealing with Stress

# Overview

If someone has an injury, for example, a broken arm, it's obvious that we can understand what has happened. But it's hard for us to recognize who has mental health issues. Sooner or later, it would do a great harm to ourselves. In this unit, we will focus on the topic of mental health at work, and learn how to deal with stress through **consulting with supervisors, asking for a transfer, leaving the job and talking about it with friends**. Now let us start our business journey!

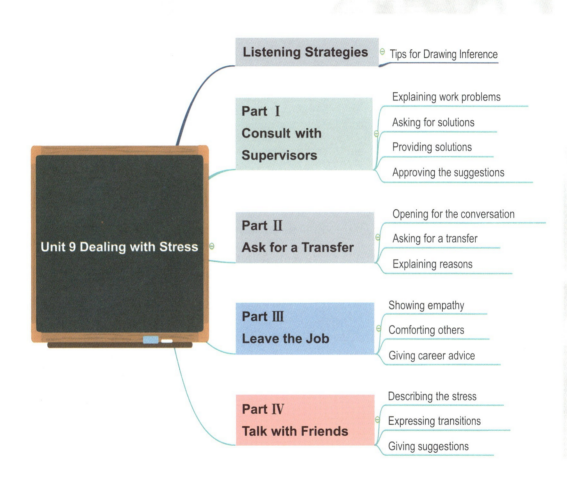

# Listening Strategies

## Drawing Inference

We've talked about strategies for listening to main ideas and details in the previous units. But sometimes, we also need to draw inference to listening conversations according to the questions. So, how can we analyze the conversation and infer the right answers?

### Tips for Drawing Inference

For listening questions that require students to "*imply*" or "*infer*" according to the conversation, the answers are definitely not obvious, at least not as other kinds of questions. In general, there are two types of inference questions.

The first one is *inferring the related words*, such as *locations*, *roles of speakers*, *job titles*, *relationships*, etc. Students might see questions like "Where did the conversation take place?". So, the first thing is to go through all the statements and choices, circle any word that is related to the concept of the conversation. And pay attention to any word that might lead you to the answer. For example, words like "treatment", "medicine" and "patient" are related to the location word, "hospital".

The second one is *inferring the speaker's purpose*. It requires students to pay attention to expressions like *in my opinion/as a matter of fact/personally*, *I think… that* that indicate the speaker's preference and feelings. And transitional words like *but*, *or* and *however* could also introduce the real purpose.

# Task ▶

Listen to the conversation and choose the correct answer for each question.

## Conversation 1

1. What is the relationship between the two speakers?

   A. Family.　　B. Classmates.　　C. Colleagues.　　D. Strangers.

2. Did the man concern about the woman?

   A. Yes.　　B. No.　　C. It didn't mention.　　D. All of the above.

## Conversation 2

1. What is the relationship between the two speakers?

   A. Family.　　B. Classmates.　　C. Colleagues.　　D. Strangers.

2. What can be inferred about the first speaker?

   A. He loves his job.　　B. He hates his job.

   C. He will miss his old job.　　D. He hasn't found the new job yet.

## Conversation 3

1. Where did this conversation take place?

   A. In the park.　　B. In the library.　　C. In the office.　　D. In the street.

2. What's the female speaker's attitude towards the male speaker?

   A. She is happy about him.　　B. She is upset about him.

   C. She is angry about him.　　D. She is concerned about him.

 **Lead-in**

## Cultural Background

Work stress is one of the most common mental health problems that happens among people at work today. Data shows that over half of people are suffering from loads of stress from their jobs. The reasons that might cause work stress are various. Maybe you are suddenly assigned for tons of work and the deadline (最终期限) is due that night. Or perhaps you are getting unfair treatment (处理; 对待) from your boss, or you just can't get along with your colleague who is everything but a team player (具有团队精神的人). Work stress can be various and it comes from all sides. If you can't handle (引导) it well, it will damage your mental health or even ruin your personal life. According to research, people who are under heavy work stress are more likely to have heart disease, high blood pressure and diabetes (糖尿病). So, since we are unable to free from work stress, how can we deal with it in a healthy way? Surely, you can either change the situation, or accept the situation. Find someone who might be your supervisor, your friends or family to talk about your problems, or learn to react in a healthy way. It would really help you to survive under workplace stress.

Unit 9 | Dealing with Stress 203

### Task 1 ▶

Read the above passage and answer the following questions.

1. What might cause work stress?

2. What kind of diseases can work stress bring to us?

### Task 2 ▶

Think about the following questions and discuss in small groups.

1. Have you ever experienced any kind of stress? How did you feel?

2. What can you do to deal with work stress?

# Warm-up

### Task ▶

There are some common reasons that might cause stress at work in the box below. Based on your own ideas and put them in the order from "Not stressful" to "Most stressful" in the scale of 1 to 5. Share the results and list the "top 3 causes of stress at work" in your group. Discuss about why you think they can cause work stress.

**Common causes of stress at work**
- Unfair treatment
- Difficult colleagues
- Heavy workload
- Terrible working environment
- Poor salary

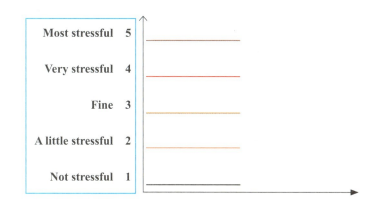

**Top 3 causes of stress at work**

1. _____ ; Reasons: _____

2. _____ ; Reasons: _____

3. _____ ; Reasons: _____

# Business Communication

## Part I Consult with Supervisors

In this part, you will hear a business conversation between a man and a woman. They talk about some workplace problems and come up with some solutions. This part consists of 3 activities. After each listening task, some useful language points will be discussed and you might use them in the following speaking task.

| **Words and Expressions** | | | |
|---|---|---|---|
| productive | /prəˈdʌktɪv/ | a. | producing or capable of producing (especially abundantly) 能生产的；生产的，生产性的 |
| agenda | /əˈdʒendə/ | n. | a list of the items that have to be discussed at a meeting 议程；日常工作事项；日程表 |
| catch up | | | to reach the point where one should be after a delay 赶上；赶做；补做 |
| task force | | | a group of people working together on a particular task (执行特定任的)工作组；特别小组 |
| keep on track | | | to ensure that you know what is happening or has happened to someone or something 保持正常进行 |

### Activity 1　Extensive Listening

Listen to the conversation and decide whether the following statements are true (T) or false (F).

1. They came to an agreement at the end of the conversation. 　　　　(　)
2. The man has some work problems that he needs to talk about. 　　　(　)
3. The man and the woman are working in the same company. 　　　　(　)

# Unit 9 | Dealing with Stress

## Activity 2 | Intensive Listening

### Task 1

Listen to the conversation and answer the following questions.

1. Did the task force work as scheduled?
2. Are the weekly meetings OK for the woman?
3. How can the problems be fixed according to the woman?

### Task 2

Listen to the conversation again and fill in the blanks with no more than three words.

A: Thank you so much for agreeing to meet with me. It will only be _____.

B: Glad to do it. You said you had some _____ about the task force?

A: Yes. So… we're not really going as scheduled. We're a little bit behind.

B: Really? That's, that's news to me.

A: Yeah. So, you see, we started out a little bit _____ and just now we're trying to play catch up and it's not really _____.

B: OK, and how are your weekly meetings? Are those OK?

A: Um… not really. You see the room keeps changing. People come in late or leave early. We really don't know what's happening and it's just really hard for everyone to be on the same page.

B: I can see that. Now how do you think we could _____ it?

A: Well, you see, right now everyone's in charge which really means no one's in charge. I've written down a few things if I can go over that with you. So, I think that if you appointed someone just to be in charge of the administrative tasks, like, for example, let's see, getting a room set up or _____ with everyone before hand, and setting up an agenda or keeping us on track during the meetings, then we can be a lot more productive.

B: I can see that. Let's _____.

A: Thank you so much for meeting with me.

## Activity 3  Speaking

### Language Bank

There might be some circumstances where you have some serious work problems, like working with difficult colleagues. And you can only solve them by consulting with your supervisor, or the HR department. Here are some expressions you might use.

**Explaining work problems:**

We're not really going as scheduled/a little bit behind.

We started out a little be slow.

We are trying to play catch-up.

It's not really working.

It's (just) really hard for everyone to be on the same page.

**Asking for solutions:**

How do you think we could fix it?

What are your suggestions?

**Providing solutions:**

I've written down a few things if I can go over that with you.

If you can..., then we can be a lot more productive.

**Approving the suggestions:**

I can see that.

Let's look into it.

Use the expressions above. Create your own business conversation and practice it with your partner.

### Situation

Role No. 1  You're the head of your work group and some of your group mates are delaying the project.

Role No. 2  You're the market director and your subordinate is under lots of pressure because of the project.

# Part II  Ask for a Transfer

In this part, you will hear a business conversation between the employee and the employer. Some serious problems seem to be hard to work out between them. This part consists of 3 activities. After each listening task, some useful language points will be discussed and you might use them in the following speaking task.

## Words and Expressions

| | | | |
|---|---|---|---|
| transfer | /trænsˈfɜː(r)/ | n. | someone who transfers or is transferred from one position to another（地点的）转移；（工作的）调动 |
| frankly | /ˈfræŋklɪ/ | ad. | expressing an opinion or feeling to emphasize that you mean what you are saying, especially when the person you are speaking to may not like it 坦率地说；老实说 |
| get along | | | to have smooth relations（勉强）生活；进展；与……和睦相处 |

## Activity 1  Extensive Listening

Listen to the conversation and decide whether the following statements are true (T) or false (F).

1. Mr. Sutcliffe is not busy right now. ( )
2. Mr. Sutcliffe disagreed with his employee's request. ( )
3. The employee is asking for a job transfer. ( )
4. The employee is having problem with the salary. ( )

## Activity 2  Intensive Listening

### Task 1

Listen to the conversation again and answer the following questions.

1. What did the female employee ask for Mr. Sutcliffe?
2. What are the reasons of the female employee's request?
3. How did Mr. Sutcliffe respond to her request?

### Task 2

Listen to the conversation again and fill in the blanks with no more than three words.

A: Is it _____ for me to come in now, Mr. Sutcliffe?

B: I'm pretty busy.

A: But…

B: All right, come in. What can I do for you?

A: Do you mind if I _____?

B: _____. Take a seat. Now what can I do for you?

A: I want to _____ the department. Do you think I could put in for a _____?

B: Yes. But why should you want to do that?

A: Do you mind if I speak frankly?

B: Not at all. _____.

A: You see, I don't like the office. I don't like the staff. And I'm afraid you and I don't get on. So, may I _____ for a transfer?

B: Yes. I'd be delighted if you did.

### Activity 3 — Speaking

## Language Bank

When there are too much work pressure coming from your current position, one of the choices is asking for a transfer or even a resignation that might give you a new beginning at work. Here are some common expressions you can use.

**Opening for the conversation:**

Is it alright for me to come in now?
Do you mind if I sit down?

**Asking for a transfer:**

Do you think I could put in for a transfer?
I want to lose the department.

**Explaining reasons:**

I don't like…
I'm afraid… don't get along.
I no longer feel attached to this place.
I want to be in a different environment.
I don't want to be stuck in a rut. I want to move on.

Unit 9 | Dealing with Stress 209

Use the expressions above. Create your own business conversation and practice it with your partner.

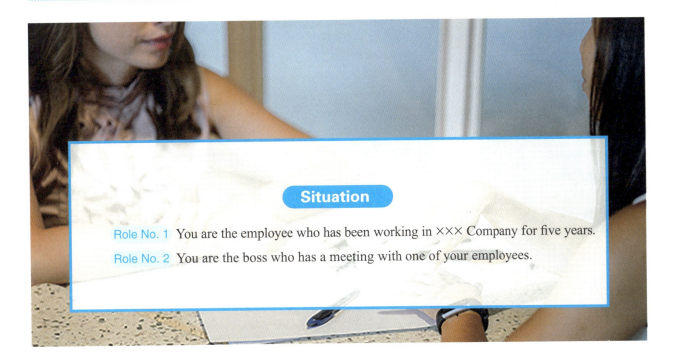

**Situation**

Role No. 1 You are the employee who has been working in ××× Company for five years.
Role No. 2 You are the boss who has a meeting with one of your employees.

# Part III  Leave the Job

It's an emotional day for Denise who's leaving Tip Top Trading company. Her colleague, Anna, is trying to comfort her and give her some career advice. Let's watch a short video and see how Anna offering help to someone who is upset and under pressure.

| Words and Expressions | | | |
|---|---|---|---|
| guidance | /ˈɡaɪdns/ | n. | help and advice 指导，引导；领导 |
| unemployed | /ˌʌnɪmˈplɔɪd/ | a. | people who are involuntarily out of work 失业的；未被利用的 |
| register | /ˈredʒɪstə(r)/ | v. | to put your name on an official list, in order to be able to do that thing or to receive a service 登记；注册 |
| thoughtful | /ˈθɔːtfl/ | a. | If you describe someone as thoughtful, you approve of them because they remember what other people want, need, or feel, and try not to upset them. 考虑周到的；体贴的；关切的 |
| brilliant | /ˈbrɪliənt/ | a. | of surpassing excellence 杰出的；有才气的；精彩的 |
| recruitment agency | | | a business that is paid to find suitable workers for other companies and organizations 招聘机构 |

| Activity 1 | Extensive Watching |

Watch a short video and answer the following questions.

1. Did Paul go out and comfort Denise?
2. Why was Denise crying?
3. Did Denise feel better after talking with Anna?

| Activity 2 | Intensive Watching |

Watch the video again and choose the correct answers.

1. Where can Denise sign up for job-finding websites?
   A. The job section of the newspaper.
   B. The recruitment agency.
   C. The Tip Top Trading.
   D. All of the above.
2. How can Denise find another job according to Anna?
   A. Look in the newspaper.
   B. Ring the contacts.
   C. Register with a job agency.
   D. All of the above.

Task 2

Watch the video again and fill in the blanks.

Anna: Denise, are you OK? Are you upset about leaving?

Denise: Yes. I've loved working here. I've made some good friends… like you Anna… Oh, and being able to make _____ phone calls has been good. What am I going to do now?

Narrator: Oh, dear Anna. It sounds like Denise needs some _____.

Anna: Career advice?

Narrator: She needs some guidance on what to do next and where to find another job. What would you do in her situation?

Anna: Look in the newspaper, ring my contacts, register with a job agency?

Narrator: Exactly! I'm sure you can give her some good advice. Go on, give it _____!

Anna: OK, I'll try. Cheer up, Denise, you need to think positively.

Denise: Do I? I'm unemployed from tomorrow, how am I ever going to find another job?

Anna: Well, have you tried looking in the job section of the _____?

Denise: No.

Anna: It's a good place to start. And there are loads of job-finding websites you could sign up for.

Denise: I don't have a _____.

Anna: Well what about _____ some of the people you know; contacts who may know about a job.

Denise: Hmm, I hadn't thought about that.

Anna: And of course, you could register with a recruitment agency. They're good at finding jobs for you.

Denise: Oh, that's a good idea. Anna, you're brilliant! What great ideas… you're so kind and… thoughtful.

Paul: Anna could you… Oh no, she's crying again.

Tom: Oh no, shall we go back into your _____, Paul?

Anna: No, no. It's OK. Denise is crying with _____. She's feeling better now.

Paul: Oh well, in that case… shall we all gather round and officially say goodbye to Denise.

## Activity 3　Speaking

### Language Bank

It's quite common today that some people might lose their jobs. And it might cause a lot of pressure when having no clues about one's future career. For this situation, you can use some common expressions as follows.

**Showing empathy:**

Are you upset about leaving?
Are you OK?
Is there anything I can do for you?

**Comforting others:**

You need to think positively.
Cheer up.

**Giving career advice:**

Have you tried (doing)…? /What about…?
You could/might want to…
It's a good place/point to start.
Try to look in the job section in the newspaper/by ringing some of the people you know/by registering with a recruitment agency.
There are loads of job-finding websites you could sign up for.

## Task 1

Use the expressions you've just learned as prompts and watch the video again. Then practice the conversation with your partner.

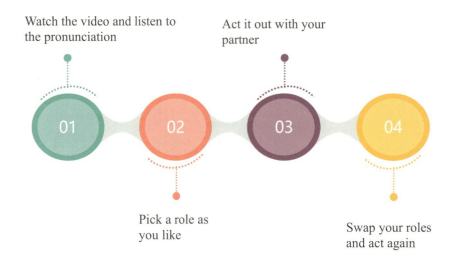

01 — Watch the video and listen to the pronunciation
02 — Pick a role as you like
03 — Act it out with your partner
04 — Swap your roles and act again

## Task 2

Use the expressions above. Create your own business conversation and practice it with your group members.

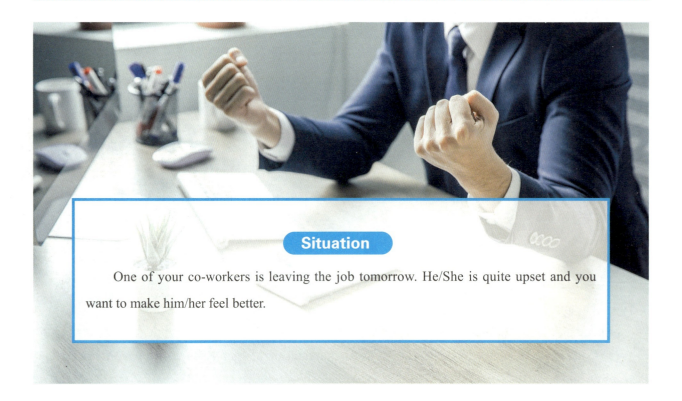

**Situation**

One of your co-workers is leaving the job tomorrow. He/She is quite upset and you want to make him/her feel better.

# Part IV  Talk with Friends

In this part, you will watch a short video about Nat Miles from Mind, and Nicola Oliver from Centre for Mental Health, talking about symptoms of mental health problems and how employers can build a mentally healthy workplace. Listen to their conversation and finish the tasks.

### Words and Expressions

| | | | |
|---|---|---|---|
| tearful | /ˈtɪəfl/ | a. | If someone is tearful, their face or voice shows signs that they have been crying or that they want to cry. 有泪的；想哭的 |
| depression | /dɪˈpreʃn/ | n. | a mental state in which you are sad and feel that you cannot enjoy anything, because your situation is so difficult and unpleasant 沮丧；忧愁；抑郁症 |
| presenteeism | /ˌpreznˈtiːɪzəm/ | n. | the practice of persistently working longer hours and taking fewer holidays than the terms of one's employment demand, especially as a result of fear of losing one's job 出勤主义 |
| breakdown | /ˈbreɪkdaʊn/ | n. | If you have a breakdown, you become very depressed, so that you are unable to cope with your life. 精神崩溃；故障；分解 |
| overt | /əʊˈvɜːt/ | a. | open and observable; not secret or hidden 明显的；公然的；蓄意的 |
| symptoms | /ˈsɪmptəms/ | n. | A symptom of an illness is something wrong with your body or mind that is a sign of the illness. 症状；症候 |
| nagging | /ˈnægɪŋ/ | n. | continually complaining or faultfinding 唠叨；挑剔 |
| reticent | /ˈretɪsnt/ | a. | temperamentally disinclined to talk 沉默的；有保留的；谨慎的 |
| empathy | /ˈempəθɪ/ | n. | understanding and entering into another's feelings 共情能力；感同身受；共鸣 |
| panic attack | | | a sudden attack of fear 惊恐发作（一种病症） |

## Activity 1  Extensive Watching

Watch a short video and answer the following questions.

1. How many people in the UK are dealing with anxiety, depression or stress according to Nat?
2. Can mental health problems affect people's performance in the workplace?
3. Who had a mental breakdown in 2007?

## Activity 2　Intensive Watching

### Task 1

Watch the video again and choose the correct answers.

1. What are the signs that an employee is becoming unwell?

   A. Becoming tearful occasionally.

   B. Having panic attacks.

   C. Difficult to concentrate in meetings.

   D. All of the above.

2. What should a manager do when his/her employees are having mental problems?

   A. Do nothing about it.

   B. Be empathy and listen.

   C. Tell them to stop nagging on their responsibilities.

   D. Fire them.

### Task 2

Watch the video again and fill in the blanks.

A: So, we know that mental health is now the _____ cause of sickness absent in the UK and we also know that one in six workers is dealing with anxiety, depression, or stress right now. So, as well as people being out of work because of a mental health problem, there's the kind of presenteeism and there's people in work who are mentally unwell and that can affect their _____ or how they're able to cope in the workplace _____. What are the signs that an employee is becoming unwell?

B: I had a breakdown in 2007. And in the build-up towards that, there's some quite overt, and symptoms that I think that my managers _____ aware of. I had too many projects going on, not enough resources… Uh, but what my line manager would have seen was somebody's been very productive. Sending emails late at night and being the first person up in the morning, taking on too many tasks. And then the symptoms started become _____. I find it very difficult concentrate in meetings. I've become a little bit tearful occasionally. I started having panic attacks. And then I got to a point where I told my line manager that I was _____ and I needed to reduce my workload. He said, no, you have to stop the nagging on your responsibilities. And _____, the symptoms got awful, a lot worse. I ran my car off the road while having a panic attack, and I was no longer able to _____ my workload. So, I took time off, time off sick.

## Activity 3 | Speaking

### Language Bank

One of the best ways to deal with workplace stress is to find someone to talk about the problems. You can use some common expressions as follows.

**Describing the stress:**

I have a break down in/when I was…

I have too many projects going on/too much workload.

I started having panic attacks.

I've become (a little bit) tearful/emotional occasionally.

I was no longer able to (cope with/deal with/continue)…

**Expressing transitions:**

At that point…

I got to a point where…

**Giving suggestions:**

I think we have to be… about…

The right way to… is…

A really good place to start is (just) to…

### Task 1 ▶

Use the expressions you've just learned to complete the following conversation. Then practice it with your partner.

A: How have you been lately? You seem _____.

B: Frankly, I'm not doing well. I have too much _____. I found myself _____. I was no longer able to _____. So, I took some time off.

A: I'm sorry to _____. I think you have to _____.

B: That sounds nice.

A: And a really good place to _____ is _____.

B: Thank you for your _____. You are so _____.

A: You're welcome.

## Task 2

Use the expressions above. Create your own business conversation and practice it with your group members.

### Situation

You are under lots of pressure from work and your best friend has invited you to hang out at his/her place. You talk about your stress and he/she gives you some advice.

Unit 9 | Dealing with Stress

# Project-based Task

## Objectives

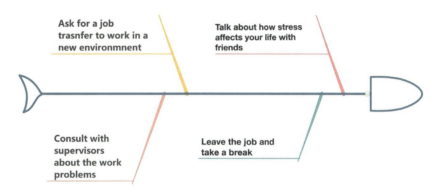

## Task Background

Susan is under a lot of pressure at work recently. She's been assigned with too much work and some of them are not even her responsibilities. She plans to talk to her supervisor and the HR department and see if it works. Her friends heard about this and are worried about her mental conditions. So, they invite her out for a drink and have a chat.

## Procedures

| | | |
|---|---|---|
| Planning |  | Discuss with group members and plan at least 3 scenarios. |
| Creating |  | Create conversations for the scenarios based on the expressions in this unit. |
| Acting |  | Choose the role you like and act out the conversations. Present the conversations in the class and make a vlog. |
| Assessing |  | Make assessment. It includes teacher's assessment (30%), self-assessment (10%), group assessment (20%), peer assessment (20%) and social assessment (20%). |

## Possible Scenarios

### Scenario 1

Susan made an appointment with her supervisor, the market director who is the head of her department. She is going to talk about some recent problems that appeared at work.

Role No. 1 Susan: Talk about problems at work

Role No. 2 Market director: Ask questions

…

### Scenario 2

Things did not go well after the meeting with her supervisor. So, Susan is going to have a meeting with the HR manager and asking for a transfer. Hopefully, it's a new start.

Role No. 1 Susan: Ask for a transfer

Role No. 2 HR manager: Ask questions

…

### Scenario 3

Susan and her friends are sitting in a coffee shop. They show their concerns for Susan and Susan tells them about the problems and stress she's been going through at work.

Role No. 1 Susan: Talk about stress and problems

Role No. 2 Susan's friend 1: Ask questions

Role No. 3 Susan's friend 2: Give advice

(Role No. 4 Susan's friend 3)

…

Requirements:

- All group members are required to take part in the project.
- Use the expressions you have learned in this unit as many as possible.

Unit 9 | Dealing with Stress

# Self-assessment Checklist

Now, it's time for you to review your performance after learning this unit. Carry out a self-assessment by checking the following table.

| Items | | Ratings | | | |
|---|---|---|---|---|---|
| | | A | B | C | D |
| Listening Skills | I can draw inference when listening to the conversation. | | | | |
| | I can infer the related words. | | | | |
| | I can infer the speakers' purpose. | | | | |
| | I can understand the explanation of work problems. | | | | |
| | I can understand the suggestions for solving work problems. | | | | |
| | I can understand advice for career development. | | | | |
| | I can understand the description of work stress. | | | | |
| | I can understand others' comfort when I'm stressed. | | | | |
| Speaking Skills | I can explain work problems. | | | | |
| | I can ask for advice and solutions. | | | | |
| | I can explain the reasons for job transfer. | | | | |
| | I can introduce other people in the business party. | | | | |
| | I can comfort others during the conversation about stress. | | | | |
| | I can provide career advice. | | | | |
| | I can describe the stress in workplace. | | | | |
| | I can use transitional words when I talk. | | | | |
| Professional Skills | I can consult with supervisors when there are stressful problems. | | | | |
| | I can ask for a job transfer appropriately. | | | | |
| | I can deal with the situation when someone leaves the job. | | | | |
| | I can have an open-ended conversation with someone about work stress. | | | | |

A: Basically agree

B: Agree

C: Strongly agree

D: Disagree